LAURENCE BONNET

T0270140

The wonderful world of
ROSE MINUSCULE

18 WHIMSICAL ANIMAL FRIENDS TO SEW

SEARCH PRESS

First published in English in 2023
by Search Press Limited
Wellwood, North Farm Road,
Tunbridge Wells, Kent TN2 3DR

First published in French in 2021 as
Le monde poétique de Rose Minuscule
Copyright © 2021 Éditions Eyrolles, Paris, France

Graphic design and layout: Lauriane Tiberghien
All photographs and illustrations are the author's own, other than
the diagrams on pages 12 to 15, which are by Lauriane Tiberghien

ISBN: 978-1-80092-103-0
ebook ISBN: 978-1-80093-094-0

The Publishers and author can accept no responsibility for any
consequences arising from the information, advice or instructions given
in this publication.

Readers are permitted to reproduce any of the projects in this book
for their personal use, or for the purpose of selling for charity, free of
charge and without the prior permission of the Publishers. Any use of
the projects for commercial purposes is not permitted without the prior
permission of the Publishers.

Suppliers
If you have difficulty in obtaining any of the materials and equipment
mentioned in this book, then please visit the Search Press website for
details of suppliers:
www.searchpress.com

The projects in this book have been made using metric measurements,
and the imperial equivalents provided have been calculated following
standard conversion practices. The imperial measurements are
often rounded to the nearest $\frac{1}{8}$in for ease of use except in some
circumstances; however, if you need more exact measurements, there
are a number of excellent online converters that you can use. Always use
either metric or imperial measurements, not a combination of both.

Safety notice
These dolls are not designed as play dolls and, because of the small
parts involved, are not suitable for children under five years old.

INTRODUCTION

I had a solitary childhood with plenty of time to get bored, and yet I had nothing to complain about: boredom is a blessing for the creative mind! I filled my time madly drawing, cutting, sticking and sewing and inventing stories and people to keep me company. I would be delighted when, at the end of a day, I would find I had made something from next to nothing, a wonderful mix of surprise and pride blooming inside me.

As I got older, my days became much less solitary, and even, some might say, hectic! At stressful moments in life, I have always turned back to my needles, pencils and fabric. When I apply myself to repeating tiny, regular sewing stitches, it is as if time stands still. As I start to choose the materials for my next project, the turmoil around me recedes. When the expression on a face comes to life with just a few embroidery stitches, I remember my soft toys, the faithful companions of my childhood, and feel soothed.

Through this book, I would like to share these feelings with you, to invite you to explore your creativity, to take pleasure in making things by hand and to enjoy the little things.

I can already picture you in my mind's eye, following the instructions for a particular project, the tip of your tongue poking out in concentration. Perhaps you are making a gift for a child? A precious object, created with patience and love, something with meaning that will be handed down from one generation to the next? Or maybe it is just for you? Something that will reconnect you with your inner child and ignite joy? Perhaps it will be a project you work on with someone else, with snacks to accompany the fun and laughter? You will give and receive encouragement and support – this is how wonderful memories are made. There goes my imagination again! I hope that yours will be sparked by this book, giving you the opportunity to reconnect with your inner child.

CONTENTS

BEFORE YOU BEGIN...

8

MATERIALS

9

TECHNIQUES

10

Basic needlework instructions · Basic crocheting
instructions · Basic knitting instructions · Specific techniques

ROSIE AND MINI-RABBIT

36

Rosie the rabbit · Mini-rabbit ·
Mini-rabbit's bed · The mattress · The blanket

THE RAINBOW CLUB FRIENDS

48

LOULOU **56** · The jumpsuit ·
The rainbow badge · The coloured pencils ·
The art portfolio · The rabbit hat

COCO **62** · The midi-skirt · The boots ·
The retro jumper · The bow headband

JEANNE **68** · The shawl ·
The sweetheart-neckline dress ·
The lacy tights · The pointy hat

BILLIE **74** · The ankle boots · The leaf
headband · The pompom scarf ·
The halterneck dress

OLIVIA **80** · The snap-fastened
cardigan · The dungarees ·
The pompom headband ·
The tote bag

BEFORE YOU BEGIN...

Take a few minutes to read these tips – they will come in handy when you are bringing to life the characters who inhabit these pages.

Some of the projects are on a very small scale. Don't let this put you off! The smallest shapes can be sewn stitch by stitch, using the manual wheel on your machine rather than the pedal. A simple pair of jewellery pliers or tweezers will help you turn the characters the right way out and stuff them without difficulty. Remember to take your time – this is the secret of success when working with tiny pieces – and take pleasure in each stage of the process!

Making a character

The pattern pieces for the characters are actual size.
Follow the instructions below on how to use them.

1 Be sure to identify all the parts you will need to make your chosen character.

2 Trace or photocopy them, preferably on to some stiff paper.

3 Make sure you also transfer the positioning of any gaps and markings (these will be transferred to the back of the fabric later in the instructions, unless stated otherwise).

4 Cut out the pattern pieces.

5 Once you have identified the grain of your fabric (see page 12), you can start making your character, following the instructions given for each project.

Happy sewing!

Making fabric clothes

The patterns for the clothes are actual size.
Hem and seam allowances are included.
Precise measurements are given in each case.
Follow the instructions below on how to use them.

1 Be sure to identify the parts of the pattern you will need for the relevant piece of clothing.

2 Trace them onto tissue paper or other thin paper, such as greaseproof paper. Draw any pieces that do not have patterns on to the thin paper, in accordance with the dimensions shown at the start of the instructions.

3 Transfer any markings.

4 Cut out the pattern pieces.

5 Identify the grain of your fabric (see page 12).

6 Fold the fabric as shown on the cutting diagram, with right sides together.

7 Position the various pieces of paper as shown on the relevant cutting diagram. For pieces that are cut on the fold, position the side marked by a dotted line along the fold of the fabric. For pieces without a pattern – for example the 11 × 64cm (4¼ × 25¼in) rectangle for the dress of the little girl hare, the first measurement (in this case 11cm/4¼in), should always run in the direction of the grain.

8 Pin around the edges of the paper pattern pieces, ensuring that the pins go through both layers of fabric.

9 Cut out the fabric around the paper pattern pieces. Remove the pins. Now you can start making your item of clothing by following the instructions.

For more details of the different techniques used in this book, see the Techniques section on page 10.

Happy sewing!

MATERIALS

Tracing/transferring
× Tissue paper
× Stiff paper
× Pencil
× Gel pen or white pencil
for dark-coloured fabrics
× Soluble fabric stabilizer
× Sewing pins

Sewing/embroidery
× Sewing machine
× Sewing needles
× Safety pin
× Iron
× Interfacing (single-sided and
self-adhesive water soluble,
iron-on, double-sided iron-on)
× Sewing thread
× DMC cotton
embroidery thread
× Metallic embroidery thread
× Flat elastic
× Hat elastic

Cutting
× Pair of sewing
scissors
× Pinking shears
× Cutter or
small scalpel

Turning out/stuffing
× Needle-nose pliers
× Chopstick or pencil
× Toy filling
× Stuffing
pellets or rice

Assembling/
sticking
× Long, pointed
needle
× Cotton cordonnet
crochet yarn
× Shirring elastic
× Mini clothes pegs
× Paper glue
× Glue gun

Knitting/
crocheting
× Knitting
needles
× Crochet hook
× Darning needle
× Marker rings
(or paperclips)
× Cotton crochet
or knitting yarn
× Pearl cotton
no. 8

Make-up
× Foam applicator
× Apricot and
pink blusher

TECHNIQUES

This technical section gives step-by-step instructions for all the basics that you will need in order to sew the characters in this book; as well as how to embroider their faces; and crochet, knit or sew their clothes and accessories.

A final section sets out some special tips that may come in handy when working on the projects in this book. They will make your work easier and ensure attractive results.

~~~~~

BASIC NEEDLEWORK INSTRUCTIONS

Identifying the grain of the fabric

The grain is the warp thread, it is parallel to the selvedge of the fabric. If you pull at your fabric, the less stretchy edge is its selvedge. The grain is, therefore, parallel to this edge. The grain line (GL) is marked by an arrow on the patterns.

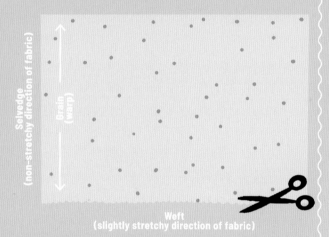

Selvedge (non-stretchy direction of fabric)

Grain (warp)

Weft (slightly stretchy direction of fabric)

Topstitching

Topstitching creates a decorative finish that is visible on the right side of the work. As a result, the stitching must be very straight and even. It is stitched using a sewing machine. For an attractive finish, you do not oversew to start or finish. It is preferable to work in the threads on the back of the work and knot them together.

For some projects in this book, you will need to topstitch to hold the seam allowances against the back of the work.

Tacking (basting)

Tacking (basting) temporarily holds work together. Sew large straight stitches by hand.

Using slip stitch to sew up a gap

Slip stitches are sewn by hand using a single thread in the same colour as the fabric.

1 Insert the needle on the wrong side of the work, a short distance before the start of the gap, bringing it out on the right side at the start of one of the folded edges of the gap (A).

2 Insert the needle through the other folded edge of the gap, just opposite the point where you brought out your thread in the previous step (B). Bring the needle back out 2mm (⅟₁₆in) further along this folded edge (C).

3 Insert the needle back through the first folded edge of the gap, just opposite the point at which you brought out your thread (D). Bring the needle back out 2mm (⅟₁₆in) further along the first folded edge (E).

4 Repeat the same step along the full length of the gap.

For a successful, almost invisible finish, you need to form even stitches and only pass the needle through the folds on the inside of the gap.

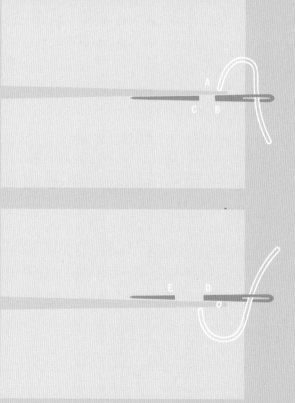

Slip stitch.

12

Making a row of gathers

Set your sewing machine to the longest straight stitch with low thread tension. Do not oversew at the start or finish, and leave a length of thread at each end.

Hold one end of the bobbin thread in one hand (the thread on the reverse side of the fabric) and push the fabric gently along it with the other hand to create the gathers. Do the same from the other side, holding the other end of the bobbin thread and arrange the folds evenly.

Sewing two lines of parallel gathers will ensure attractive, even gathering. This is the process you should follow each time an instruction includes making gathers.

Overcasting

Overcasting prevents the edges of fabric from fraying. Make sure you don't skip this step: it will ensure that the characters' clothes are nicely finished, hard-wearing and the correct size.

Overcasting can be done with an overlocker if you have one, but you can also use the zigzag stitch setting on a household sewing machine, as is the case here.

Each time overcasting is used in the instructions for making clothes, set your machine as follows: zigzag stitch – stitch length: 1mm (1⁄16in) – stitch width: 4mm (3⁄16in)

Sewing/embroidering running stitch

Running stitch can be decorative or can be used to hold fabric in place. It is used to tack (baste) by hand or to embroider the whiskers of certain characters, among other things. It is done by hand as follows:

1 Insert the needle on the wrong side of the fabric and bring it out on the right side.

2 Insert the needle again, a little further along the line you are working, forming the first stitch, and bring it out again on the wrong side.

3 Insert the needle a short distance from the first stitch, along the line you are working, bringing it out a little further along to form the second stitch.

4 Repeat until the end of the line you are working. The stitches should be very even when used for embroidery.

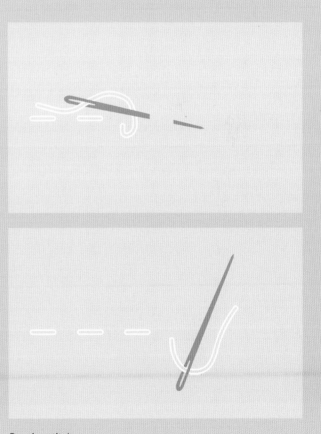

Running stitch.

Sewing/embroidering backstitch

Backstitch is used for assembly or decoration. It allows you to create continuous lines, without the spaces you get in running stitch. It is used here to embroider the eyes, nose and mouth of certain characters.

It is done by hand as follows:

1 Insert the needle on the wrong side of the work and bring it out at A on the right side.

2 Insert the needle at B, at a point a short distance behind A then bring out the needle at C, a point a little way beyond A.

3 Insert the needle again at A, and bring it out at D, a point a little way beyond C.

4 Continue in the same way along the whole line you are working.

If you are sewing round a curve, use smaller stitches to achieve a more attractive end result.

Embroidering French knots

The French knot is a decorative stitch. It is used here to embroider some of the characters' eyes and freckles.

It is done by hand as follows:

1 Insert the needle on the wrong side of the fabric and bring it out on the right side.

2 Hold the thread taut and wrap it twice around the needle.

3 Insert the needle as close as possible to the place where it first came out, holding the wrapped yarn tight and pressing it against the fabric.

4 Pull the needle through, keeping your thread taut.

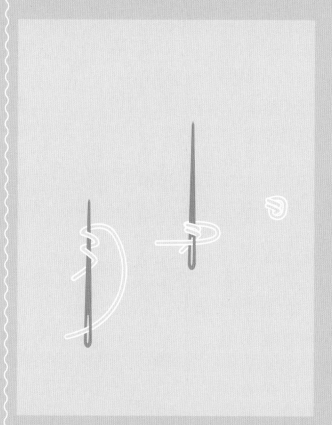

Backstitch.

French knots.

Embroidering
straight stitch

This embroidery stitch consists of individual stitches forming a broken line. It is used to embroider the lines on the foreheads of the cat characters.

It is done by hand as follows:

1 Insert the needle on the wrong side of the fabric, bringing it out on the right side and reinserting it a little further on to form the first stitch.

2 Bring out the needle on the right side and insert it a little further on to form the second stitch.

3 Continue in the same way across the whole of the area you are working.

Embroidering
satin stitch

This embroidery stitch uses a series of straight stitches, sewn parallel and adjacent to each other to fill in a small area. It is used to embroider the noses of characters.

It is done by hand as follows:

1 Insert the needle at A, from the wrong side to the right side of the work.

2 Insert the needle at B, and bring it out at C, very close to A.

3 Insert the needle at D, very close to B.

4 Continue until you have completely filled the whole area you are working. The stitches should be neatly parallel to each other.

Straight stitch.

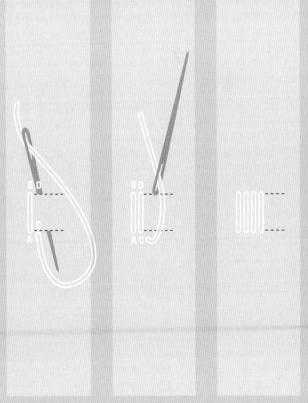

Satin stitch.

BASIC CROCHETING INSTRUCTIONS

Form a slipknot to start

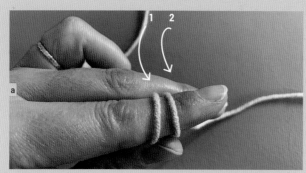

1 Wrap the yarn twice around your index finger (**a**).

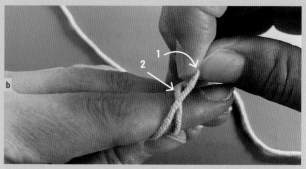

2 Pass loop 1 over loop 2: the two loops are still around your index finger (**b**).

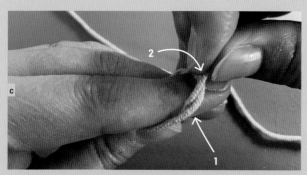

3 Pass loop 2 over loop 1 and off the end of your index finger: only loop 1 is still on your finger (**c**, **d**).

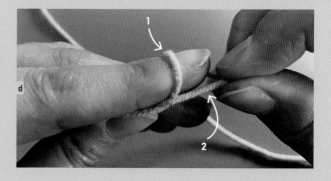

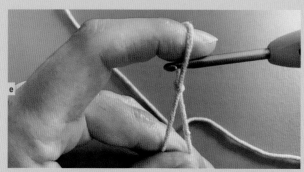

4 Gently, draw tight.

5 Transfer the loop you have made to your crochet hook (**e**). Pull gently so the loop on the crochet hook is taut but not too tight.

UK/US crochet stitch conversions

Only UK crochet terms are used in the patterns throughout this book. For US conversions, please refer to the following terms:

UK		US	
dc	double crochet	**sc**	single crochet
htr	half-treble crochet	**hdc**	half-double crochet
tr	treble crochet	**dc**	double crochet
tension	gauge		
adjustable ring	magic ring		

Making a chain

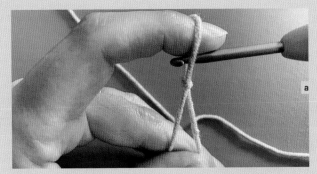

1 Form a slipknot to start (a).

2 Wrap the yarn round the hook (b).

3 Draw the yarn that is round the hook through the loop on the crochet hook (c, d, e). You have formed a chain stitch (ch).

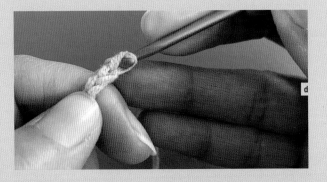

4 Make as many chain stitches as required (f). You have formed a chain.

The pictures above show a chain that has already been started, so you can see the process more clearly.

Double crochet (dc)

1 Insert the hook through the stitch of the previous round or in the chain (**a**, **b**).

2 Yarn round hook (**c**).

3 Draw the yarn that is round the hook through the stitch of the previous round to the front of the work: you now have two loops on the hook (**d**).

4 Yarn round hook again (**e**).

5 Draw the yarn that is round the hook through the two loops on the crochet hook. You have formed a double crochet (**f**, **g**, **h**).

Slip stitch (sl st)

1 Insert the hook through the stitch of the previous round or in the chain (a).

2 Yarn round hook (b).

3 Draw the yarn round the hook through the stitch of the previous round to the front of the work: then through the loop on the hook (c, d, e). You have formed a slip stitch (sl st).

Treble crochet (tr)

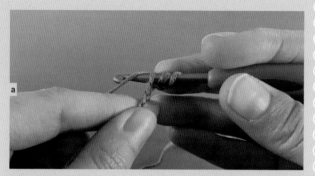

1 Yarn round hook, insert the hook through the stitch of the previous round or in the chain and repeat yarn round hook (**a**).

2 Draw the yarn through the stitch: you have three loops on the hook (**b**).

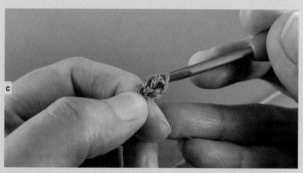

3 Yarn round hook again, draw the yarn through the first two loops on the hook: you now have two loops on the hook (**c**).

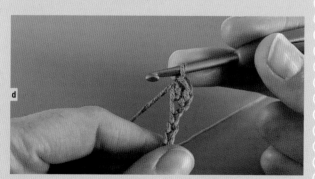

4 Yarn round hook again, draw the yarn through the two loops on the hook: you have formed a treble crochet (**d**).

Half-treble crochet (htr)

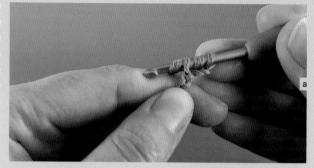

1 Yarn round hook, insert the hook through the stitch of the previous round or in the chain and repeat yarn round hook (**a**).

2 Draw the yarn through the stitch: you have three loops on the hook (**b**).

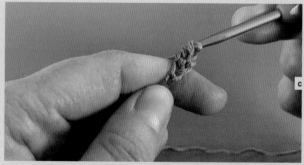

3 Yarn round hook again, draw the yarn through the three loops on the hook: you have formed a half-treble crochet (**c**).

Increasing (inc)

1 Work a stitch into the stitch of the previous round (for example a double crochet) (a).

2 Work a second stitch, inserting the hook through the same stitch of the previous round (b). You have increased by one stitch!

Decreasing (dec)

1 Insert the hook through the stitch of the previous round. Yarn round hook and draw the yarn through the same stitch: you have two loops on the hook (a).

2 Insert the hook through the next stitch. Yarn round hook and draw the yarn through the same stitch: you have three loops on the hook (b).

3 Yarn round hook and draw the thread through the three loops on the hook: you are left with a single loop on the hook (c, d). You have decreased by one stitch!

Making a chain ring

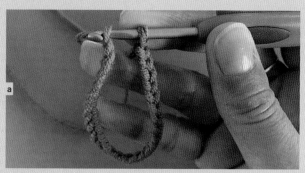

1 Work a chain. At the end of the chain, insert the hook through the first stitch of the chain (**a**).

2 Yarn round hook (**b**).

3 Draw the yarn round the hook through the two loops on the hook (**c**). You have joined the chain into a ring using a slip stitch (sl st).

Working in rounds

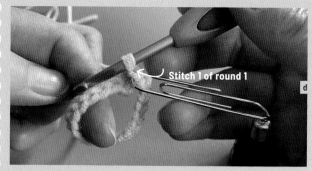

Stitch 1 of round 1

1 On a chain ring, insert a marker ring under the stitch that formed the chain into a ring. This will be the first stitch of the first round (**a**).

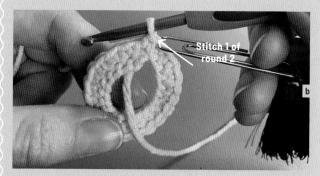

Stitch 1 of round 2

2 Crochet the first round following the instructions for the project in question.

3 Remove the marker ring to crochet the marked stitch and reposition the ring under this new stitch. This will be stitch one of round two (**b**).

4 Continue crocheting the second and subsequent rounds, repositioning the marker ring under the first stitch of each new round.

Making an adjustable ring

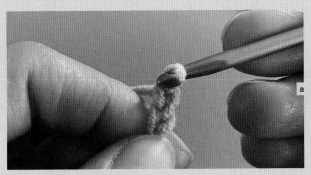

1 Work a chain of two chain stitches (a).

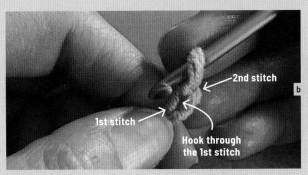

2nd stitch

1st stitch

Hook through
the 1st stitch

2 Insert the hook through the first stitch of the chain (b). Work a double crochet.

3 Work five further double crochets, continuing to insert the hook through the first stitch of the chain: you now have a round of six stitches (c).

4 Crochet the second round, following the instructions for the project in question, marking the first stitch of the round with a marker ring (d).

5 Pull gently on the yarn at the base of the adjustable ring: the adjustable knot draws tight and the hole formed disappears (e). Continue the work.

Changing colour

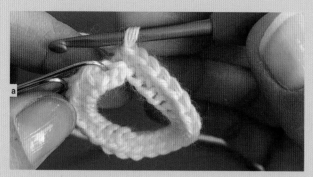

1 Crochet all the stitches of the round in your first colour, in this case white (**a**).

2 In the next round, insert the hook through the first stitch of the previous round. Yarn round hook, still using the white yarn (**b**).

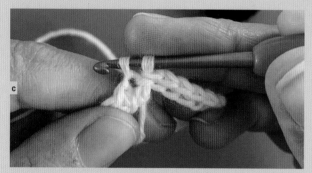

3 Draw the yarn through the stitch: you have two white loops on the hook (**c**).

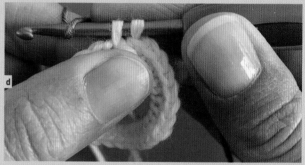

4 Yarn round hook with the yarn in your second colour, in this case blue (**d**).

5 Draw the yarn round the hook through the two white loops (**e**). You have a blue loop on the hook and the first stitch of the second round is white.

6 Mark this first stitch with a marker ring and crochet all the stitches of the round in the second colour (**f**). To work the third round in white, follow the instructions given in step 2, reversing the colours.

BASIC KNITTING INSTRUCTIONS

Casting on

Casting on is done on a single needle.

1 Form a slipknot to start (see page 16). You need to leave a good length of yarn before the knot – I will call this length the 'tail' in the following instructions.

2 Transfer the slipknot to the knitting needle.

3 Place the yarn attached to the ball to the RH side of the needle and the tail to the left of the needle.

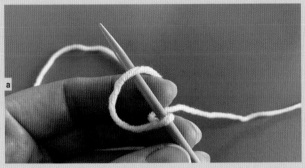

4 Pass the tail to the right, over the needle. The yarn forms a loop to the left of the needle (**a**).

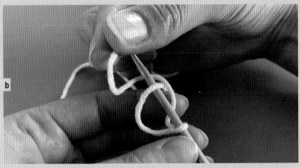

5 Pass the yarn attached to the ball behind the needle and over the loop (**b**).

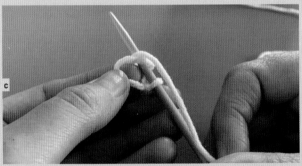

6 Hold the loop and pass it over the end of the needle (**c**, **d**). You have formed a stitch.

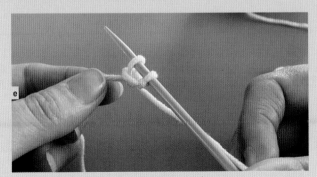

7 Pull on the tail, then the yarn attached to ball to adjust the stitch around the needle. The stitch should be neither too tight nor too loose on the needle (**e**).

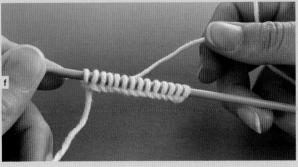

8 Repeat this step as many times as the project requires (**f**). The stitches should be nice and even.

Knit stitch (k)

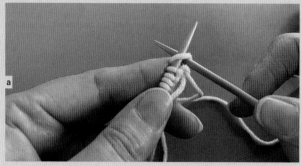

1 Insert the RH needle (with no stitches) through the first stitch, passing it under the LH needle (a).

2 Pass the yarn attached to the ball around the RH needle, wrapping it under then over. The yarn is then between the two needles (b, c).

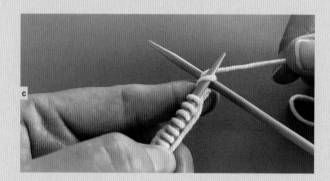

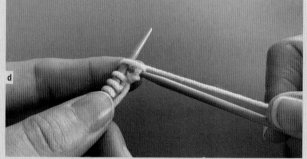

3 Turn the point of the RH needle gently downwards and bring it back on top of the LH needle (d, e).

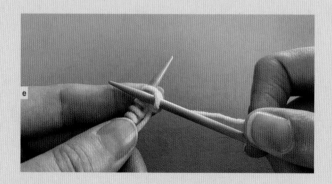

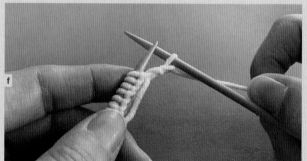

4 Let the stitch on the LH needle slip off, holding the others in place with your index finger. There is now a new stitch on the RH needle. You have formed a knit stitch (f).

5 Continue in the same way with all the stitches on the LH needle. You have formed a row of knit stitch.

Purl stitch (p)

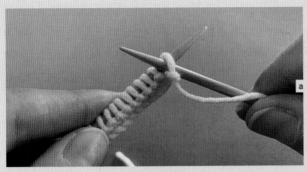

1 Insert the RH needle (with no stitches) through the first stitch, passing it over the LH needle (**a**).

2 Wrap the yarn attached to the ball around the RH needle, wrapping it over the needle, from right to left. The yarn is then between the two needles (**b**, **c**).

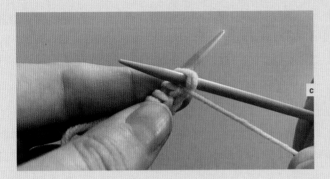

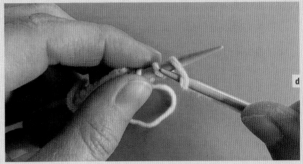

3 Turn the point of the RH needle gently downwards and bring it back under the LH needle (**d**).

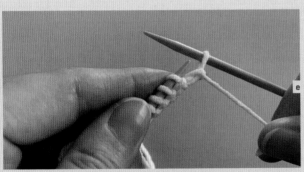

4 Let the stitch on the LH needle slip off, holding the others in place with your index finger. There is now a new stitch on the RH needle. You have formed a purl stitch (**e**).

5 Continue in the same way with all the stitches on the LH needle. You have formed a row of purl stitch.

Increasing

To increase, you need to knit in the same stitch twice: a knit stitch followed by a purl stitch.

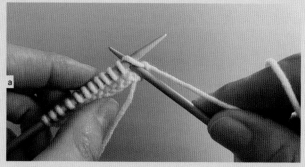

1 Insert the RH needle through the stitch, passing it over the LH needle (a).

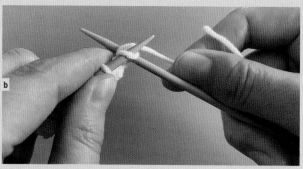

2 Pass the yarn attached to the ball around the RH needle, wrapping it under then over. The yarn is then between the two needles (b).

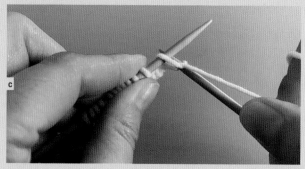

3 Turn the point of the RH needle gently downwards and bring it back on top of the LH needle (c, d). Do not drop the stitch from the LH needle!

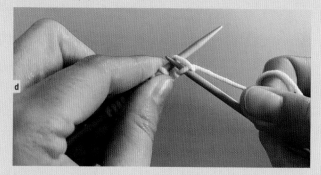

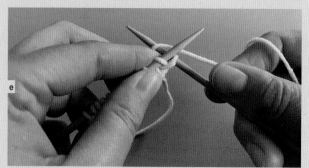

4 Reposition the RH needle behind the LH needle (e) and bring the yarn attached to the ball between the two needles, at the front of the work.

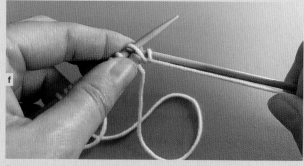

5 Insert the RH needle through the stitch, passing it over the LH needle (f).

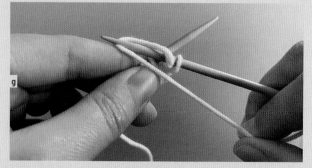

6 Wrap the yarn attached to the ball around the RH needle, wrapping it over the needle, from right to left. The yarn is then between the two needles (g).

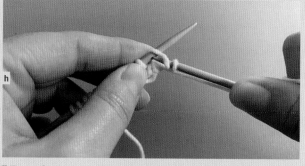

7 Turn the point of the RH needle gently downwards and bring it back under the LH needle (h).

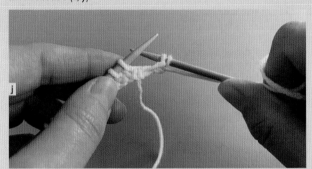

8 Let the stitch on the LH needle slip off, holding the others in place with your index finger. You have worked an increase (**i**, **j**).

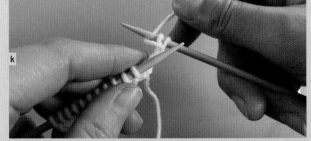

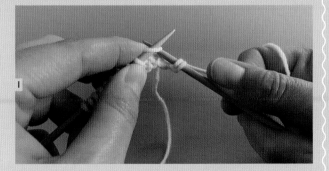

9 Replace the yarn attached to the ball at the back of the work and knit the rest of the row using knit stitch (**k**, **l**).

Decreasing

To decrease, you simply knit two of the stitches together.

1 Insert the RH needle through two stitches, as if they were just one (**a**).

2 Knit a normal knit stitch. Drop the two stitches from the LH needle. You have worked a decrease (**b**, **c**).

Cable cast on

Picking up stitches at the edges

1 After the last row, flip the work over. Cast on at the start of the next row. Insert the RH needle between the first two stitches on the LH needle (**a**).

2 Yarn over (wrap the working yarn around the RH needle as if you are going to knit normally).

3 Use the RH needle to bring the yarn round the needle to the front of the work and transfer this new stitch to the LH needle, pulling out the RH needle (**b, c, d**).

1 Place the working yarn behind the work. Insert a crochet hook between two stitches on the edge. Use the hook to bring the working yarn to the front (**a**).

2 Transfer this loop to the knitting needle. You have picked up one stitch (**b**).

3 Insert the hook between the next two edge stitches (**c**). Bring another loop to the front of the work.

4 You have completed the first stitch of a cable cast-on. Repeat this step as many times as required.

4 Transfer the loop to the knitting needle. You have picked up two stitches (**d**). Repeat as required.

Garter stitch

Knit all the rows in knit stitch.

Stocking (stockinette) stitch

Knit all odd rows in knit stitch and all even rows in purl stitch. Also known as knit on the right side, purl on the wrong side.

Knit 2 purl 2 ribbing

Knit 2 purl 2 ribbing alternates two knit stitches then two purl stitches across the whole row. It is abbreviated to K2 p2 or 2x2 rib.

If the last two stitches of the row were knit stitches, the first two stitches of the following row should be purl stitches, then the next two knit stitches.

If, however, the two last stitches of the row were purl, the first two stitches of the following row should be knit stitches, then the next two purl.

Seed stitch

Seed stitch alternates one knit stitch and one purl stitch across the whole row.

If the last stitch of the row was a knit stitch, the first stitch of the following row should be a knit stitch, then the next a purl.

If however, the last stitch of the row was a purl stitch, the first stitch of the following row should be purl, then the next a knit.

Casting off (binding off)

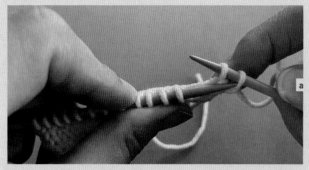

1 Knit the first two stitches of the row. Insert the LH needle into stitch one, passing it from left to right (**a**).

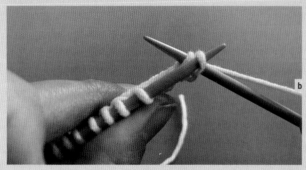

2 Lift the first stitch on the RH needle over the second stitch then drop it off the LH needle. You have cast off (bound off) one stitch (**b**, **c**).

3 Knit the third stitch. Cast off (bind off) stitch two over stitch three as previously. Continue in the same way for the whole row (**d**).

SPECIFIC TECHNIQUES

Attaching arms with cordonnet crochet yarn

1 Double thread a long, pointed needle with the cordonnet crochet yarn (other than for Lili the little mouse on page 104 and Oscar the little lion on page 120, where you will use a single thread).

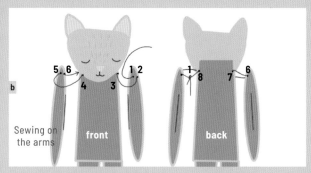

2 Place the figure facing you and position the arms on either side of the body (a).

3 With reference to diagram (b), above, and the numbered markings, proceed with the following instructions.

4 Insert the needle in the left arm at the point marked number 1 (leaving a tail of yarn 5–6cm (2–2½in) in length) and bring it out at point 2 (c). Make sure you only pass the needle through the top layer of fabric!

5 Insert the needle in the front left of the body, just under the head, at point 3 (d) and bring it out on the opposite side, at point 4.

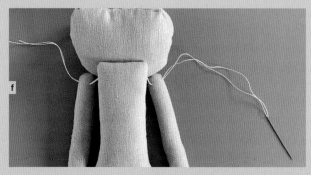

6 Insert the needle in the right arm at point 5 and bring it out at point 6 (e). Make sure you only pass the needle through the top layer of fabric!

7 Flip the figure over (f) and insert the needle on the RH side of the back of the body at point 7 and bring it out on the opposite side at point 8 (g).

8 Pull gently on both ends of the yarn to bring the arms and the body together. Use a double knot to secure the ends (**h**).

9 Trim off the ends of the yarn, 3mm (⅛in) from the knot (**i**).

Transferring pattern markings using a pin

You will need to use this technique in two circumstances:
- to transfer a point already marked on the wrong side of the fabric to the right side
- to transfer a point drawn on a paper pattern to the right side or wrong side of a piece of fabric.

In the first case:

1 On the wrong side of the fabric, insert a pin through the point to be transferred.

2 On the right side of the fabric, use a pencil to mark the point on the right side where the pin has pierced the fabric.

In the second case:

1 Place the paper pattern on the right side of the fabric, according to the positioning marks shown.

2 Insert a pin at the point to be transferred and pierce right through the paper.

3 On the fabric, use a pencil to mark the point on the right side where the pin has pierced the fabric.

Transferring face markings to the right side of the fabric using a pin

1 Use a pencil to draw the outline of the face on the wrong side of the fabric and transfer markings A, B and C, as described in the instructions for each model.

2 On the wrong side of the fabric, insert a pin through one of the three markings (a).

3 On the right side of the fabric, use a pencil to mark the point on the right side where the pin has pierced the fabric (b).

4 Do the same for the two other markings (c). These three markings, transferred to the right side of the fabric, will allow you to correctly position the faces, ears, mouths and noses of your characters.

Transferring a face design using soluble fabric stabilizer

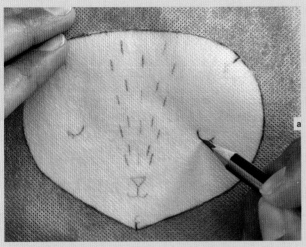

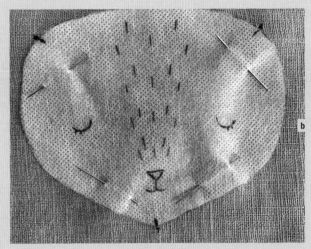

1 Place the piece of soluble fabric stabilizer over the pattern for the face. Using a pencil, trace the outline of the face, markings A, B and C, and all the lines on the face (a).

2 Cut out the stabilizer around the outline of the face.

3 Place it on the right side of the fabric, aligning markings A, B and C, and pin to hold in place (b).

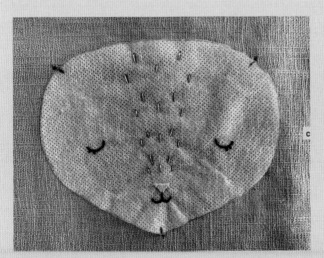

4 Start to embroider according to the instructions for the particular character, embroidering over the facial features and sewing through the two layers of fabric (c).

5 When you have finished embroidering, dip the fabric in some warm water to dissolve the stabilizer. Rub gently (d).

6 Place the embroidered face between two layers of towelling (terrycloth) and press to absorb any excess water. Leave to dry.

Rosie and Mini-rabbit

MATERIALS

Finished size of Rosie: 30cm (11¾in) with ears upright • Mini-rabbit: 8cm (3¼in)
See pages 45 and 47 for patterns and illustrations.
For more details of the techniques used, see the Techniques section on page 10.
The instructions for Mini-rabbit's bed also apply to Mina the little cat's chest.
The measurements marked 🐰 are just for Mini-rabbit's bed.
Those marked 🐱 are just for Mina's chest.

Rosie
× 26 × 54cm (10¼ × 21¼in) short-pile faux fur in ecru
× 18 × 20cm (7 × 7¾in) cotton voile in pale pink
× DMC embroidery cotton in black
× Sewing thread in ecru
× 20cm (7¾in) cotton cordonnet crochet yarn in white, thickness 0.3mm (⅛in)
× 2 magnets Ø 5mm (³⁄₁₆in)
× Toy filling
× Blusher in pink and apricot
× Long pointed needle
× 3 pattern pieces (body, arm, ear)

Mini-rabbit
× 10.5 × 14.5cm (4⅛ × 5¾in) cotton cordonnet crochet yarn in ecru
× 10.5 × 4.5cm (4⅛ × 1¾in) cotton voile in pale pink
× Sewing thread in black and ecru
× Short length of thread in metallic gold
× Toy filling
× Bell Ø 7mm (¼in)
× Blusher in pink and apricot
× Flat jewellery pliers (or another long, thin tool)
× 2 pattern pieces (body, ear)

🐰 Mini-rabbit's bed/🐱 Mina's chest
× 🐰 22 × 20cm (8¾ × 7¾in)/🐱 50 × 52cm (18 × 20½in) light brown card
× 1 sheet of stiff paper
× 🐱 80cm (31½in) ribbon, 1cm (⅜in) wide
× Ruler
× Pencil
× Scissors
× Paper glue
× Mini clothes pegs
× 🐰 2 illustrations for the bed
× 🐱 2 illustrations for the box

The mattress
× 12 × 9cm (4¾ × 3½in) striped cotton fabric (or cretonne, linen, poplin or similar)
× Sewing thread to match chosen fabric
× Toy filling

The blanket
× 5-ply (sport) woollen knitting yarn in grey-blue
× Knitting needles 3.5mm (UK 9/10, US 4)
× Darning needle
× Stitches used: decorative stitch alternating k3 p3

Come, my little one, into my loving arms.
Snuggle up against my heart and
my soft fur will keep you warm.

ROSIE THE RABBIT

See the list of materials on page 36.

CUTTING AND TRACING DIAGRAM

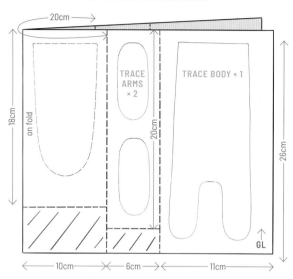

1 Following the cutting diagram, cut the faux fur into five pieces:
- 2 pieces 26 × 11cm (10¼ × 4¼in) for the rabbit's body
- 2 pieces 20 × 6cm (7¾ × 2½in) for the arms
- 1 piece 18 × 20cm (7 × 7¾in) for the ears.

The ears

2 Trace the outline of the ear twice on the wrong side of the pale pink cotton voile, leaving an allowance of at least 1cm (⅜in) outside the traced lines, except at the base of the ears.

3 Place this rectangle of fabric on the piece of faux fur of the same size, right sides together. Stitch round the traced outline of the ears, leaving the base of the ears open (red line).

4 Cut round the ears, 4mm (³⁄₁₆in) from the seams and directly against the openings.

5 Turn the ears the right way out. At the base of the ears, fold the sides to the middle, inside to inside (so cotton voile against cotton voile) (a).

6 Sew along the base of the ears, 1cm (⅜in) from the edge, to hold the folds in place. Set to one side.

The arms

7 On the wrong side of the pieces of 20 × 6cm (7¾ × 2½in) faux fur, trace the outline of the arms twice, leaving a seam allowance of at least 1cm (⅜in) outside the lines. Mark the position of the gaps O–O'.

8 Place this piece of fabric on the second piece of the same size, right sides together. Stitch round the arms on the lines marked, leaving the gaps.

9 Cut around the arms, 4mm (³⁄₁₆in) from the seams and the gaps.

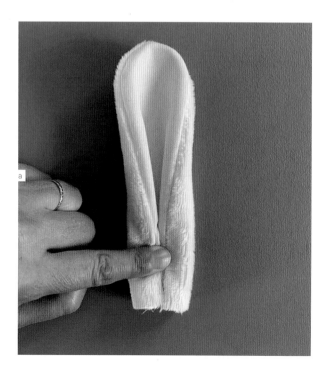

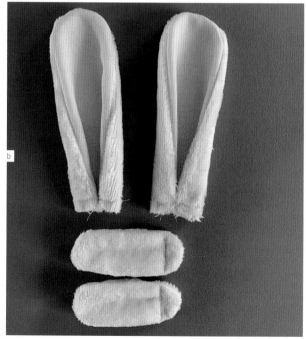

10 Turn them the right way out. Insert a magnet into each arm, pushing it to the end.

11 Secure the magnet in place by sewing crossways across the arms, next to the magnet, 1.5cm (½in) from the end: this will be the rabbit's paw.

12 Turn under 4mm (³⁄₁₆in) on either side of gaps and sew up using slip stitch (**b**). Set to one side.

The body

13 On the wrong side of one of the pieces of 26 × 11cm (10¼ × 4¼in) faux fur, trace the outline of the rabbit's body, leaving a seam allowance of at least 1cm (³⁄₈in) outside the line. Mark the position of gap O–O'.

14 Cut along the line at the top of the rabbit's head. Add markings A–A' and B–B' to mark the position of the ears.

15 Use a pin to mark the position of the eyes on the wrong side of the fabric (see technique on page 33). Use the same technique to transfer an 'M'-shaped mark to the wrong side of the fabric: this will be the starting point for embroidering the nose and the mouth.

16 Split the embroidery thread so you are only using two strands. Use this two-strand thread to embroider French knots for the eyes (see page 14).

17 Bring the same needle up through 'M', from the wrong side of the fabric. Use backstitch to embroider a U (see page 14), sticking as far as possible to the lines traced from the pattern. At this point, what you embroider is up to you! Large or small, symmetrical or a little lop-sided, your rabbit's facial features will be unique.

18 Once you have embroidered the U, embroider the mouth, just below, starting from the centre. Once again, it is up to you what sort of expression you want to give your rabbit.

Assembling the ears and the body

19 Position the front of the ears face down against the front of the face, matching markings A-A' and B-B' and aligning the stitch line holding the ears in place with the edge of the fabric at the top of the head.

20 Pin the ears to hold them in place (**c**).

21 Place this on the second piece of faux fur of the same size, right sides together. Make sure it is properly centred: the top of the head should be around 2cm (¾in) under the top edge of the fabric.

22 Pin all round the body to hold it in place. Sew around the outline of the body along the line, and 1.5cm (½in) from the top edge of the head, ensuring that you do not catch the ears in the stitches down the sides. Leave gap O-O' open.

23 Cut around your rabbit, 5mm (³⁄₁₆in) from the seams and the gap.

24 Turn your rabbit the right way out and stuff firmly.

25 Turn under 5mm (³⁄₁₆in) on either side of the gap, and sew up using slip stitch.

Attaching the arms

26 Position the arms on either side of the body, the ends with the magnets downwards. Place the top of the arms 6cm (2½in) from the top of the head.

27 Attach the arms to the body with cordonnet crochet yarn, following the instructions on page 32.

Finishing touches

28 Use the apricot blusher to add a little colour to your rabbit's nose. Use the pink blusher for its cheeks. Rosie the rabbit is complete! (**d**)

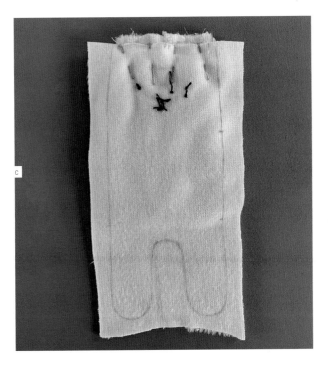

MINI-RABBIT

See the list of materials on page 36.

CUTTING AND TRACING DIAGRAM

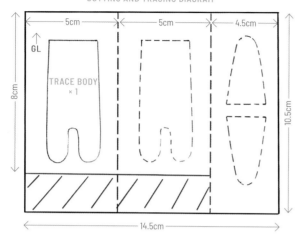

1 Following the cutting diagram, cut the cotton into three pieces:
- 2 pieces 8 × 5cm (3¼ × 2in) for the body
- 1 piece 10.5 × 4.5cm (4⅛ × 1¾in) for the ears.

The ears

2 Trace the outline of the ear twice on the wrong side of the cotton voile, leaving an allowance of at least 1cm (⅜in) outside the traced lines, except at the base of the ears.

3 Place this rectangle of fabric on the piece of cotton of the same size, right sides together. Stitch around the traced outline of the ears leaving the openings at the base of the ears open (red line).

4 Cut around the ears, 3mm (⅛in) from the seams and directly against the openings.

5 Turn the ears the right way out. At the base of each ear, fold the sides to the middle, inside to inside, (so cotton voile against cotton voile) (a).

6 Put in a few stitches by hand to hold the base of the ears in place, 3mm (⅛in) from the edge (b).

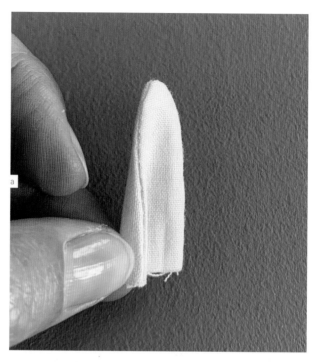

When you are barely 8cm (3³/₈in) tall, you can feel very small, fragile and insignificant.
But don't be fooled: this little rabbit is much bolder than he looks!

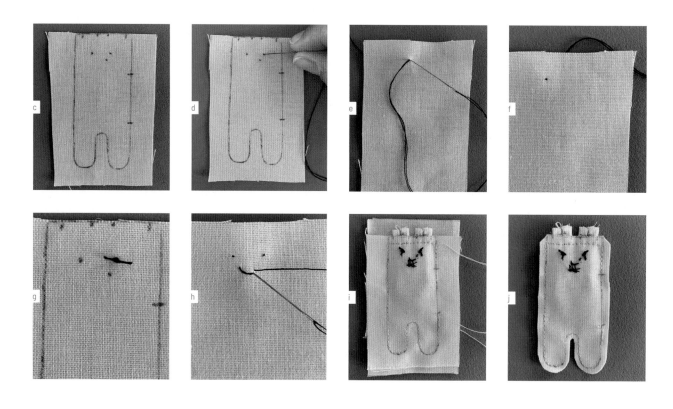

The body and head

7 On the wrong side of one of the pieces of 8 × 5cm (3¼ × 2in) cotton, trace the outline of the rabbit's body, leaving a seam allowance of at least 1cm (⅜in) outside the lines. Mark the position of gap O–O'.

8 Cut along the line at the top of the rabbit's head. Transfer markings A–A' and B–B' to mark the position of the ears.

9 Use a pin to mark the position of the eyes on the wrong side of the fabric (see technique on page 33). Use the same technique to transfer marking M to the wrong side of the fabric: this will be the starting point for embroidering the nose and mouth (**c**).

10 Using doubled black thread, and without tying a knot, insert the needle at the position of one of the eyes, from the back to the front of the fabric (**d**). Leave a long tail of thread. Insert the needle again, in the right side of the fabric, just next to where it came out (**e**). Pull gently (**f**).

11 Knot the ends of the thread together on the wrong side of the fabric. Trim off the threads 2mm (¹⁄₁₆in) from the knot (**g**).

12 Do the same for the second eye.

13 Using a single black thread, bring the needle up through marking M, from the wrong side of the fabric. Use backstitch to embroider a U for the nose (**h**). At this point what you embroider is up to you! Large or small, symmetrical or a little lop-sided, your rabbit's facial features will be unique.

14 Once you have embroidered the U, embroider the mouth, just below, starting from the centre. Once again, it is up to you what sort of expression you want to give your Mini-rabbit.

Assembling the ears and body

15 Place the embroidered fabric on the second piece of the same size, right sides together. Make sure it is properly centred: the top of the head should not be too close to the top edge (about 1cm/⅜in).

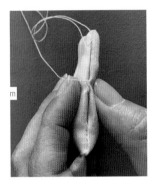

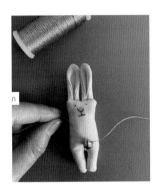

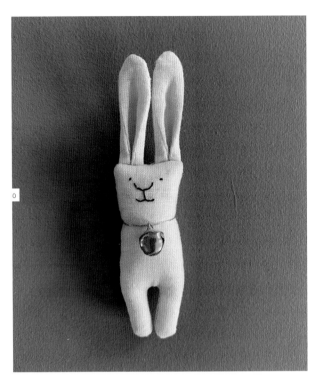

16 Start sewing along the outline of the body from marking O'. When you are 4mm (³⁄₁₆in) from Mini-rabbit's top edge, lift the presser foot of your sewing machine and place one ear between the two pieces of fabric, between marks A–A'. Position the front of the ear face down against the front of the face, aligning the stitch line holding the ears in place with the edge of the fabric at the top of the head.

17 Sew along top of Mini-rabbit's head, 4mm (³⁄₁₆in) from the edge. When you reach marking B, lift the presser foot to insert the second ear and continue in the same way.

18 Continue along the stitch line until you reach marking O (**i**).

19 Cut around Mini-rabbit 3mm (⅛in) from the seam and the opening, ensuring you do not cut off the base of the ears where they stick through inside the head. Clip the corners on either side of the top of the head (**j**).

20 Carefully turn Mini-rabbit the right way out, first pulling out the ears and then turning the legs the right way out one by one. You can use jewellery pliers to help (**k**).

21 Stuff Mini-rabbit, starting with the legs (**l**).

22 Turn under 3mm (⅛in) on either side of the gap, and sew up using slip stitch (**m**).

Finishing touches

23 Use the apricot blusher to add a little colour to your rabbit's nose. Use the pink blusher for its cheeks.

24 Thread the little bell on to a length of gold thread and tie it around the rabbit's neck (**n**).

Mini-rabbit is complete! (**o**)

MINI-RABBIT'S BED/ MINA'S CHEST

See the list of materials on page 36.
The instructions below can be used to make both these things.

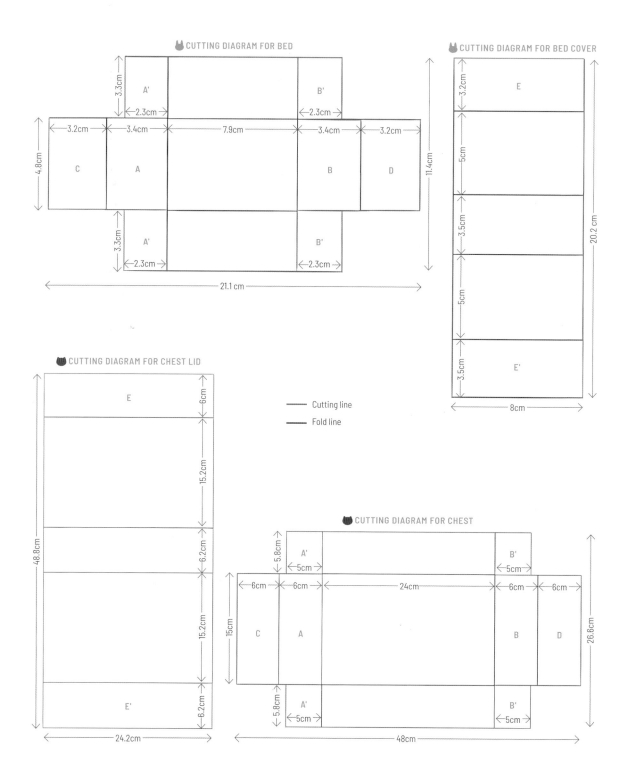

CUTTING DIAGRAM FOR BED

CUTTING DIAGRAM FOR BED COVER

CUTTING DIAGRAM FOR CHEST LID

CUTTING DIAGRAM FOR CHEST

—— Cutting line
━━ Fold line

1 Using the diagrams on the facing page, copy the two parts of the bed/chest on to the back of the cardboard.

2 Cut out the two pieces, following the blue cutting lines (**a**).

Constructing the base of the box

3 Using a ruler, mark the folds shown in pink on the back of the cardboard (**b**). Crease the folds using your thumbnail (**c**). Each part is folded wrong side to wrong side.

4 Turn the base of the box upside down, so the outside is facing you. Glue the four rectangles marked A' and B' on the diagram (**d**). Fold the glued tabs against the internal faces of rectangles A and B (**e**).

5 Glue the inside surfaces of C and D. Fold the glued tabs down against the internal faces of A–A' and B–B' (**f**).

6 Hold the glued ends together with mini clothes pegs and leave to dry (**g**).

Constructing the lid

7 Glue the inside face of rectangle E of the lid and stick it against the external face of rectangle E' (**h**).

8 Hold the glued end together with mini clothes pegs and leave to dry.

Decorating the box

9 Choose one of the two illustrations suggested 🐰 below/ 🐰 on page 144, and print your favourite on a stiff piece of paper. Cut out.

10 Glue the back and stick it on the top of the box cover, ensuring that it is nicely centred.

11 Close the box, by sliding the base into the cover.

The bed/chest is complete!

My rabbit

lucky-charm

Hello little rabbit

You can download these illustrations at actual size from
www.bookmarkedhub.com

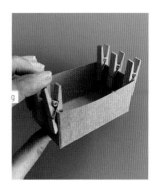

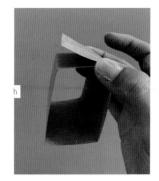

THE MATTRESS

See the list of materials on page 36.

1 Cut the cotton fabric rectangle into two 6 × 9cm (2½ × 3½in) pieces. Place one on top of the other, right sides together.

2 Add markings 2.5cm (1in) from each end on one of the long sides. These markings indicate the position of the 4cm (1½in) gap.

3 Sew around the mattress, 5mm (³⁄₁₆in) from the edge, leaving the gap open, and clip the corners (**a**).

4 Turn the mattress the right way out and stuff.

5 Turn under 5mm (³⁄₁₆in) on either side of the gap and sew up using slip stitch.

6 Use doubled sewing thread, without a knot, to create the mattress effect. To do so, push the needle through the central point of the rectangular mattress, leaving a long tail of thread on the other side. Push the needle back through, right next to where it came out (**b**) and pull the thread through the mattress. Repeat three times. Tie the ends of the thread together in a tight double knot. Trim the threads flat against the knot (**c**).

7 Repeat in the four corners of the mattress, 1cm (⅜in) from the edges (**d**).

The mattress is complete! Place it in the bottom of the box (**e**).

THE BLANKET

See the list of materials on page 36 and the Basic knitting techniques on pages 25–31.

1 Cast on 18 sts.

Rows 1–3: *k3 p3*, repeat three times.

Rows 4–6: *p3 k3*, repeat twice.

Rows 7–9: as rows 1–3.

Rows 10–12: as rows 4–6.

Rows 13–15: as rows 1–3.

Row 16–19: as rows 4–6.

Rows 19–21: as rows 1–3.

Row 22: cast off (bind off).

2 Fasten off and snip yarn ends.

The blanket is complete!

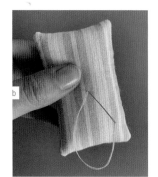

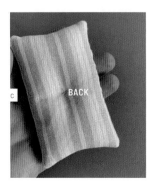

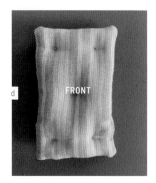

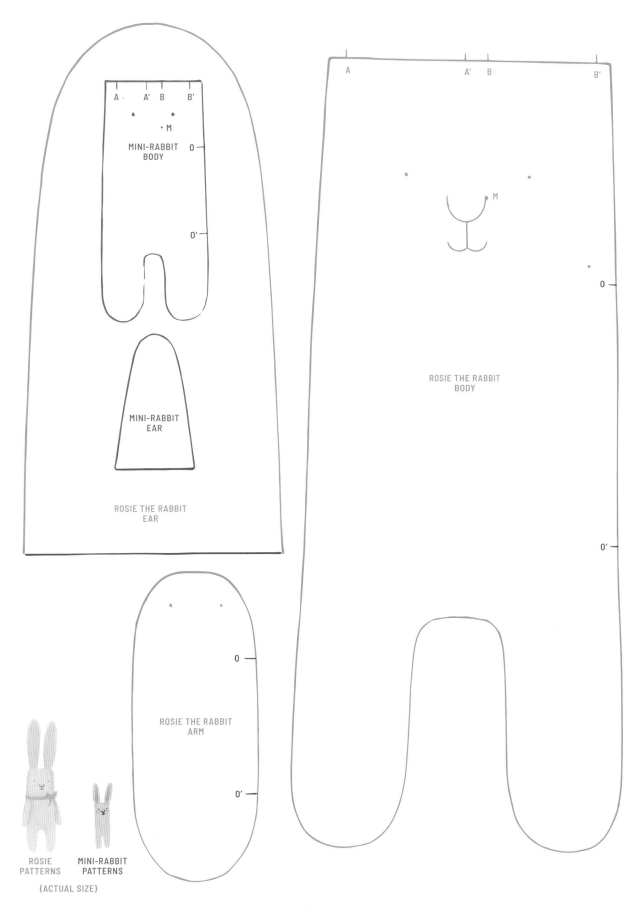

A   A'   B   B'

• M

MINI-RABBIT
BODY

MINI-RABBIT
EAR

ROSIE THE RABBIT
EAR

A   A' B   B'

• M

ROSIE THE RABBIT
BODY

ROSIE THE RABBIT
ARM

ROSIE
PATTERNS

MINI-RABBIT
PATTERNS

(ACTUAL SIZE)

47

The Rainbow Club Friends

MATERIALS

Finished size: 34cm (13½in)
See pages 86–89 for patterns.
For more details of the techniques used, see the Techniques section starting on page 10.
The instructions for making the big cats are the same as for the little cat Mina.
Likewise, Jeanne's shawl also works for Mina's shawl and Jeanne's pointy hat is the same as the
one worn by Marcel the bear and Tom and Emilie, the hares.
Follow the symbols given in the materials section and the instructions.

🐱Big cats and 🐱little Mina
× 🐱 28 × 75cm (11 × 29½in) linen in grey (Loulou), ecru (Coco), dark grey (Jeanne), sky blue (Billie) or beige (Olivia), depending on the character chosen
× 🐱 10 × 19cm (4 × 7½in) plain cotton in peach
× 🐱 30 × 10cm (11¾ × 4in) faux fur (tail)
× 🐱 Sewing thread in black, pink and to match the colour of the linen
× 🐱 Embroidery thread in metallic gold or sewing thread in rust, blue, turquoise or garnet depending on the character chosen (see page 52)
× 🐱 14 × 10cm (5½ × 4in) soluble fabric stabilizer
× 🐱 18 × 46cm (7 × 18in) linen in grey
× 🐱 7 × 12cm (2¾ × 4¾in) plain cotton in pale pink
× 🐱 9 × 8cm (3½ × 3⅛in) soluble fabric stabilizer
× 🐱 2 × chenille stems, each measuring 20cm (7¾in)
× 🐱 Sewing thread in black, pale pink and grey
× 🐱 Embroidery thread in metallic gold
× 30cm (11¾in) cotton cordonnet crochet yarn, 0.3mm thick, in grey
× Long pointed needle
× Toy filling
× 5 pattern pieces (head, body, arm, leg, ear)/ 🐱 + 1 pattern piece (tail)

Loulou's jumpsuit
× 36 × 37cm (14 × 14½in) cotton (or poplin, polycotton, cretonne or similar) in blue lagoon
× 42cm (16½in) very fine elastic, such as hat elastic
× Sewing thread to match chosen fabric
× 2 shop-bought pompoms, Ø 2cm (¾in), in white
× Safety pin
× 2 pattern pieces (leg, top) + 1 ruff to trace

Loulou's rabbit hat
× 16 × 34cm (6¼ × 13½in) short pile faux fur in ecru
× 16 × 18cm (6¼ × 7in) cotton in peach
× 10 × 15cm (4 × 6in) double-sided fusible interfacing
× 4 × 2.6cm (1½ × 1in) single-sided fusible interfacing
× Sewing thread in ecru
× 3 pattern pieces (ear, hat, hat edge)

Loulou's art portfolio
× 14 × 9cm (5½ × 3½in) thin cardboard
× 17.5 × 9cm (7 × 3½in) leatherette in midnight blue
× 15cm (6in) round elastic, Ø 2mm (1⁄16in), in gold
× Mini clothes pegs

Rainbow badge
× 1 sheet of thick paper
× Badge or brooch pin
× Strong glue
× Scissors
× Rainbow illustration (see page 59)

Loulou's colouring pencils
× 5 × 7cm (2 × 2¾in) fabric
× 8 wooden skewers, such as kebab sticks, Ø 4mm (3⁄16in)
× Small amount of acrylic paint in 8 different colours
× Short length of cordonnet crochet yarn
× Scrap of sandpaper
× Fine paintbrush
× Wire cutters

Coco's midi-skirt
× 15 × 46cm (6 × 18in) broderie anglaise fabric in eucalyptus
× 20cm (7¾in) round elastic, Ø 1mm (1⁄16in)
× Sewing thread to match fabric
× Safety pin

Coco's retro jumper
× 4-ply (fingering) knitting wool, in mustard yellow
× Small button, Ø 8mm (5⁄16in) (vintage or otherwise)
× Sewing thread in mustard yellow
× Knitting needles 3mm (UK 11, US 2/3)
× Crochet hook 3mm (UK 11, US 2/3) hook
× Stitches and techniques used: k2 p2 ribbing • single rib (k1 p1) • increase (inc) • decrease (dec) • cable cast on • picking up stitches at the edges

Coco's boots
× 2 rectangles, 7 × 8cm (2¾ × 3¼in), of leatherette in dark brown
× Sewing thread in dark brown
× 1 pattern piece (boots)

Because they are stronger together, they set up the Rainbow Club.
And who are they? Meet Loulou, Coco, Olivia, Billie and Jeanne.
Five girls with very different personalities and interests who support
and help each other in the most cheerful fashion!

Coco's bow headband
× 9 × 44cm (3½ × 17½in) fine, lightweight fabric
(cotton voile, cambric, muslin or similar) in bright green
× Sewing thread in green
× 6cm (2½in) flat elastic, 5mm (³⁄₁₆in) wide

Jeanne's sweetheart-neckline dress
× 24 × 62cm (9½ × 24½in) printed cotton (or poplin, cretonne,
polycotton or similar)
× 2 lengths of round elastic measuring 10cm (4in),
Ø 2mm (¹⁄₁₆in), in gold
× 1 snap fastener Ø 7mm (¼in)
× Sewing thread to match chosen fabric
× Small amount of toy filling
× Tapestry needle
× 1 pattern piece (bodice) + 1 skirt to draw

🐱Jeanne and 🐱Mina's shawl
× 5-ply (sport) knitting wool, in 🐱écru/🐱green
× Knitting needles 4mm (UK 8, US 6)
× Darning needle
× Stitches used: garter stitch • increase (inc)
× 🐱DMC embroidery thread in navy blue
× 🐱Short length of DMC embroidery thread in bronze
× 🐱Small piece of strong cardboard

Jeanne's lacy tights
× 2 pieces of 26.5 × 11.5cm (10½ × 4¼in) fine stretch lace
× 2 pieces of 26.5 × 11.5cm (10½ × 4¼in) soluble fabric stabilizer
× 15cm (6in) very flexible round hat elastic or 30cm
(11¾in) shirring elastic in white, to be folded in half
× Safety pin
× 1 pattern piece (leg)

The pointy hat worn by 🐱Jeanne 🐱Marcel and both 🐱Tom and Emilie
× 🐱6 × 10.5cm (2⅜ × 4⅛in)/🐱5 × 5cm (2 × 2in)/🐱6.5 × 6.5cm
(2½ × 2½in) leatherette, in gold, or thick, sequinned material
× Sewing thread to match the chosen fabric
× Shirring elastic in gold
× 🐱Shop-bought pompom, Ø 1.5cm (½in)
× 🐱🐱5-ply or 8-ply (sport or DK) knitting wool (around 6m/6½yd)
× 🐱🐱Fork
× 🐱🐱Scissors
× Thick pointed needle
× Glue gun
× 1 pattern piece (pointy hat, see page 89/100)

Billie's halterneck dress
× 28 × 52cm (11 × 20½in) printed fabric (cotton, cambric,
poplin or similar)
× Sewing thread to match chosen fabric
× 2 pieces of 18cm (7in) ribbon, 6mm (¼in)
wide, in colour matching chosen fabric
× 10cm (4in) flat elastic, 5mm (³⁄₁₆in) wide
× Small piece of thin cardboard (from a cereal box, for example)
× Safety pin
× 5 pattern pieces (skirt, front bodice, back bodice, pocket,
pocket pattern in cardboard) + 1 ruffle to draw

Billie's ankle boots
× 2 squares of 6 × 6cm (2½ × 2½in) leatherette in tan
× Sewing thread in tan
× Small amount of shirring elastic in gold
× Long pointed needle
× 1 pattern piece (boot)

Billie's pompom scarf
× 2 5-ply or 8-ply (sport or DK) knitting yarns, in pine
green and ecru
× Sewing thread in pine green
× Knitting needles 3.5mm (UK 9/10, US 4)
× Darning needle
× Large sewing needle
× Fork
× Scissors
× Stitch used: stocking (stockinette) stitch

Billie's leaf headband
× 9 × 6cm (3½ × 2½in) felt in green
× 25cm (9¾in) shirring elastic in gold
× Thick pointed needle
× Glue gun
× 2 pattern pieces (large leaf, little leaf)

Olivia's dungarees
× 27 × 24cm (10½ × 9½in) printed cotton
× Sewing thread to match fabric
× 2 pieces of 20cm (7¾in) ribbon, 6mm (¼in)
wide, in colour matching chosen fabric
× 10cm (4in) flat elastic, 5mm (³⁄₁₆in) wide
× Safety pin
× 2 pattern pieces (trousers, bib)

Olivia's snap-fastened cardigan
× 4-ply (fingering) cotton knitting yarn, in red
× Snap fastener, Ø 6mm (¼in)
× Knitting needles 3mm (UK 11, US 2/3)
× Thick sewing needle
× Stitches and techniques used: k2 p2 ribbing • stocking
(stockinette) stitch • decrease (dec) • increase (inc)

Olivia's tote bag
× 5-ply (sport) cotton knitting yarn, in sand
× 20cm (7¾in) ribbon, 6mm (¼in) wide, in green
× Crochet hook 3.5mm (UK 9/10, US 4)
× Thick darning needle
× Marker ring
× Stitches and techniques used: adjustable ring
• double crochet (dc) • slip stitch (sl st) • chain
stitch (ch) • increase (inc) • decrease (dec)

Olivia's pompom headband
× 5-ply or 8-ply (sport or DK) knitting
wool (around 6m/6½yds), in red
× 30cm (11¾in) shirring elastic in gold
× Thick pointed needle
× Darning needle
× Scissors
× Fork

THE BIG CAT AND THE LITTLE CAT

See the list of materials on page 48.
The instructions marked 🐱 are just for the big cats
and the ones marked 🐱 just for the little cat.

CUTTING AND TRACING DIAGRAM

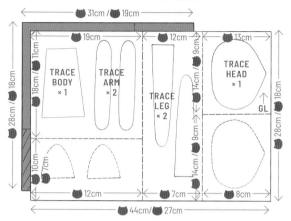

1 Following the cutting diagram, cut the linen into seven pieces:
- 2 pieces 🐱 14 × 13cm (5½ × 5in)/🐱 9 × 8cm (3½ × 3¼in) (for the head)
- 1 piece 🐱 10 × 19cm (4 × 7½in)/🐱 7 × 12cm (2¾ × 4¾in) (for the ears)
- 2 pieces 🐱 28 × 12cm (11 × 4¾in)/🐱 18 × 7cm (7 × 2¾in) (for the legs)
- 2 pieces 🐱 18 × 19cm (7 × 7½in)/🐱 11 × 12cm (4¼ × 4¾in) (for the body and arms).

The face

2 On the wrong side of the two pieces of 🐱 14 × 13cm (5½ × 5in) / 🐱 9 × 8cm (3½ × 3¼in) linen, trace the outline of the head once, leaving a space of at least 1cm (⅜in) outside the line. Transfer markings A, B and C and the position of gap O–O' (**a**).

3 Transfer markings A, B and C to the right side of the fabric, using the pin method (see page 34).

4 Trace the face design on to the piece of soluble fabric stabilizer (see technique on page 35) (**b**, **c**).

5 Embroider the face, starting with the eyes, in backstitch using doubled black thread. Continue by embroidering the outline of the nose in backstitch, using doubled pale pink thread. Then fill in the muzzle using satin stitch, worked vertically, hiding the outline that you embroidered in the previous step. Next embroider the mouth, in backstitch, using doubled black thread (**d**).

For **Jeanne**, **Loulou** and 🐱 **the little cat Mina**, embroider the lines on their foreheads in running stitch, using single gold thread (**e**).

For **Olivia**, embroider the freckles on her cheeks, using French knots, with doubled rust thread. Embroider the lines in straight stitch with doubled blue thread (**f**).

For **Coco**, embroider the stripes in straight stitch with doubled garnet thread, and the whiskers with single gold thread (**g**).

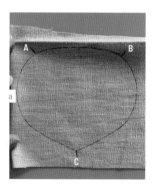

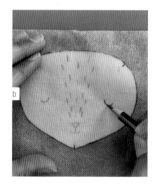

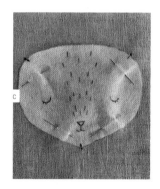

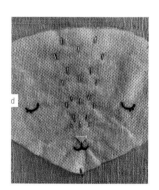

JEANNE

OLIVIA

COCO

BILLIE

For **Billie**, embroider the stripes in straight stitch with doubled turquoise thread, and the whiskers with single gold thread (**h**).

6 Immerse the embroidered face in some warm water for 1–2 minutes to dissolve the fabric stabilizer, then place it between two layers of towelling (terrycloth) and press so any excess water is absorbed. Leave to dry (**i**).

You can download the embroidery patterns for the faces from www.bookmarkedhub.com

The ears

7 Trace the outline of the ear on to the wrong side of the 🐱 peach/🐱 pale pink fabric twice. Make sure you leave a seam allowance of 1cm (⅜in) between lines, except from at the base of the ears (red line).

8 Place this fabric on the 🐱 10 × 19cm (4 × 7½in)/🐱 7 × 12cm (2¾ × 4¾in) linen, right sides together. Sew around the line, leaving the base of the ears open (**j**).

9 Cut around the ears, 🐱 4mm (³⁄₁₆in)/🐱 3mm (⅛in) from the seam and directly across the base of the ears. Turn the right way out, making sure you push out the points (**k**).

Assembling the head and ears

10 Position the pattern piece on the right side of the embroidered face, aligning it with markings A, B and C. Place the ears on the pattern piece, with the inside of the ears face down, according to the markings. Pin the base of the ears to the embroidered face to hold them in place (**l**).

11 Remove the paper pattern piece. Now place the embroidered face with the pinned ears on the other piece of linen of the same size, right sides together.

12 Sew round the head on the stitch line, leaving gap O–O' between the ears open. Sew backwards and forwards a few times on either side of the gap to ensure the seam is secure.

13 Cut around the head 🐱 4mm (³⁄₁₆in)/🐱 3mm (⅛in) from the seam, avoiding the base of the ears that stick out from the head (**m**).

14 Turn the head the right way out, pushing one ear through the gap first. Next, pull gently to bring out the rest of the face, and finally the second ear (**n**).

15 Stuff the head, pushing the toy filling well into the edges of the face to make attractive curves.

16 Turn under, 🐱 4mm (³⁄₁₆in)/🐱 3mm (⅛in) on either side of the gap and sew up using slip stitch (**o**). Set the head to one side for now (**p**).

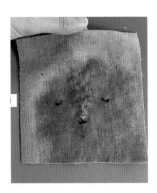

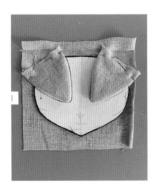
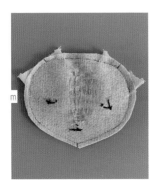

The legs, body and arms

17 On the wrong side of one of the pieces of 🐱 28 × 12cm (11 × 4¾in) / 🐱 18 × 7cm (7 × 2¾in) linen, trace the outline of the leg twice, leaving a space of at least 1cm (⅜in) outside the line, except at the base of the legs.

18 Place this piece of fabric on the second piece of the same size, right sides together. Sew the legs together along the line, leaving the openings marked with a red line at the base of the legs open.

19 Cut around the legs, 🐱 4mm (³⁄₁₆in)/🐱 3mm (⅛in) from the seams and directly against the openings. Clip the curves at the bottom of the legs.

20 On the wrong side of one of the pieces of 🐱 18 × 19cm (7 × 7½in)/🐱 11 × 12cm (4¼ × 4¾in) linen, trace the following in accordance with the cutting diagram:
• the outline of the body × 1
• the outline of the arms × 2.

Leave a space of at least 1cm (⅜in) around the lines. Mark the position of the gap O–O' for the arms.

21 Place this piece of linen on the second piece of the same size, right sides together. Sew each of the pieces together along the stitch line, leaving the base of the body (red line) open and gap O–O' for the arms.

22 Cut around the pieces, 🐱 4mm (³⁄₁₆in)/🐱 3mm (⅛in) from the seams and the gaps for the arms and directly against the opening on the body. Trim round the curves at each end of the arms with pinking shears (**q**).

23 Turn the legs, body and arms the right way out. Stuff the body and legs very firmly.

24 🐱 For the big cats:
Stuff the arms lightly so they are pliable (**r**) and set to one side for now.

24 🐱 For the little cat:
Fold one of the two 20cm (7¾in) lengths of chenille stem in half. Twist the two ends together for around 1cm (⅜in). Bend this twisted section back against the rest of the chenille stem. Place the piece of chenille stem inside the arms (see pictures **h** and **i** in the instructions for assembling Marcel the bear, page 94). Do the same for the other arm. Set the arms to one side for now.

Attaching the legs

25 Turn under 🐱 8mm (⅜in)/🐱 5mm (³⁄₁₆in) on either side of the opening at the base of the body.

26 Insert the top of one leg approximately 5mm (³⁄₁₆in) into the opening at the base of the body, positioning it against the side seam.

27 Start to sew the opening at the base of the body closed, using slip stitch, inserting the needle through the body and the leg in turn (**s**). When the first leg is attached, insert the second in the opening and finish the seam (**t**).

Attaching the head

28 Position the front of the body against the back of the head, using the marking on the pattern to guide you.

29 Sew together using slip stitch, in a single thread of the colour that matches the linen. Sew through the head and the body in turn. Leave the part under the chin unstitched (**u**). Sew backwards and forwards to ensure the seam is secure (**v**).

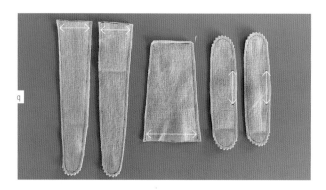
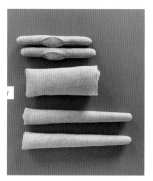

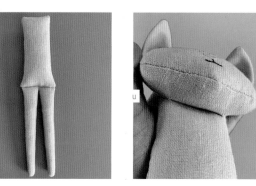
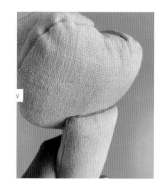

Attaching the arms

30 Turn under  4mm (³⁄₁₆in)/ 3mm (⅛in) on either side of the gap in the arms and sew up using slip stitch (**w**).

31 Attach the arms to the body with cordonnet crochet yarn, following the instructions on page 32.

The little cat is complete!

Tail

For the big cat:

32 Fold the piece of fur in half lengthways, right sides together. Trace the outline of the folded tail on the fabric, making sure that you have assembled parts 1 and 2 of the pattern to make a single piece.

33 Pin the two layers of fur together and sew along the line, leaving the base of the tail open (red line).

34 Cut around the tail, 8mm (⁵⁄₁₆in) from the seams and directly against the opening.

35 Turn the tail the right way out, making sure you push out the point.

36 Turn under 1cm (⅜in) on either side of the opening in the tail.

37 Place the tail on the back of the body, using the marking on the pattern as a guide, and pin all round.

38 Sew the tail to the body using slip stitch. The big cat is complete!

LOULOU

~

Loulou is the most creative:
she was the one who designed
the club's badge. Laid back
and dreamy, she writes and
draws cartoon scenes.

THE JUMPSUIT

See the list of materials on page 48.

1 Cut out the seven pattern pieces for the jumpsuit, following the instructions in the section Making fabric clothes on page 8 (the ruffle measures 5 × 36cm/2 × 14in).

2 Overcast the edges of all the pieces except one of the long edges of the ruffle.

The trousers

3 On the two front leg pieces, insert pins to mark A–A' and B–B'.

4 Right sides together, bring mark A to A' and mark B to B' to form tucks. Pin to secure in place and sew along the top edge of the front leg pieces, 5mm (³⁄₁₆in) from the edge.

5 Place the two front leg pieces right sides together. Sew around the crotch, 7mm (¼in) from the edge. Iron open the seams and set to one side for now.

6 Insert pins in the two back pieces to mark A–A' and B–B' as well as O–O' marking the gap for the tail.

7 Repeat the steps given in stages 4 and 5, but ensuring you leave gap O–O' open.

Assembling the top and bottoms

8 Place the front of the top and the front of the trousers right sides together. Align the edges of the bottom of the top and the top of the trousers. Pin, then stitch all along, 1cm (³⁄₈in) from the edge.

9 Do the same with the back of the top and the back of the trousers.

10 Turn under 5mm (³⁄₁₆in) along the front and back edges of the armholes. Sew along the folds, 3mm (⅛in) from the edge.

11 Turn under 5mm (³⁄₁₆in) along the front and back edges of the neckhole. Sew along the folds, 3mm (⅛in) from the edge.

12 Use a pin to mark the middle of the neckhole at the front and back. Set to one side for now.

The ruffle

13 Fold the rectangle in half widthways, right sides together. Align the edges of the two shorter sides and stitch along them 7mm (¼in) from the edge.

14 Use a pin to mark the fold line at the opposite end, then press the seam open with an iron.

15 Turn under 2mm (¹⁄₁₆in) along the long, non-overcast edge. Press with an iron to hold in place.

16 Set the stitch length on your sewing machine to 0.5mm and the width to 3mm (⅛in). Overcast with zigzag stitch along this long side to make an attractive edge.

17 Turn under 1cm (³⁄₈in) along the second long edge that has already been overcast, to form the hem for the elastic. Press with an iron to hold in place.

CUTTING DIAGRAM

```
←————— 18.5cm —————→

GL ↑

FRONT LEG          BACK LEG
  × 2                × 2                    36cm

TOP × 2

fold line     RUFFLE × 1              5cm
              ←— 18cm —→
```

Attaching the ruffle

18 Place the front and back of the jumpsuit right sides together. Insert the ruffle between the two pieces of the top, aligning the seam between the short edges of the ruffle with the middle of the back of the top (wrong side of the ruffle against right side of the top). Pin the top and the ruffle together, with the top of the ruffle extending 2mm (⅟₁₆in) beyond the top of the top (**a**).

19 Align the pin marking the fold opposite the ruffle seam with the pin marking the middle of the front of the top (wrong side of ruffle against right side of top). Pin as previously (**b**, **c**).

20 Sew round the hem of the ruffle, 7mm (¼in) from the edge, leaving a 2cm (¾in) gap at a point where it is not stitched to the top.

Finishing touches

21 Place the front and back of the jumpsuit right sides together. Pin along the sides and fold the seam allowance between the top and the trousers down against the trousers.

22 Sew along the edges of jumpsuit, 7mm (¼in) from the edge, starting from the bottom of the trousers and stopping at the bottom of the armholes. Press the seams open with an iron.

23 Turn under 1cm (⅜in) at the bottom of each trouser leg. Sew along the folds, 7mm (¼in) from the edge, to make hems for the elasticated cuffs.

24 Cut two 10cm (4in) lengths of elastic and thread through the hems.

25 Pull on the ends of the elastic to reduce the width of the cuffs to approximately 3cm (1¼in). Knot the ends of the elastic together and hide the knots in the cuffs (**d**).

26 Sew around the crotch, 7mm (¼in) from the edge, right sides together.

27 Thread the remaining length of elastic through the hem of the ruffle. Pull on the ends of the elastic to reduce the width of the ruffle to approximately 8cm (3¼in).

28 Knot the ends of the elastic together and hide the knots in the hem.

29 Sew up the gap in the hem of the ruffle using slip stitch.

30 Turn the outfit the right way out. Sew the pompoms on the front: one on the ruffle and the other below it on the stomach.

The jumpsuit is complete!

THE RAINBOW BADGE

See the list of materials on page 48.

1 Print out the badge illustration on a piece of paper at actual size.

2 Cut out the picture, leaving a small margin all around; this will make cutting easier.

3 Stick the badge pin to the back of the picture with a dab of strong glue.

The badge is complete!

You can download this illustration from
www.bookmarkedhub.com

(ACTUAL SIZE)

THE COLOURED CRAYONS

See the list of materials on page 48.

1 Use wire cutters to snip off the wooden skewers 4cm (1⁹⁄₁₆in) from the pointed end.

2 Use sandpaper to smooth off the cut ends.

3 Paint the sides of the pencils and the tip of the point to look like the coloured lead.

4 Leave to dry and add a second coat if necessary.

5 Fold the piece of fabric widthways to get a rectangle measuring 2.5 × 7cm (1 × 2¾in). Gather the pencils together and wrap the rectangle of fabric around them to form a holder.

6 Hold the fabric in place by knotting the cordonnet crochet yarn around the pencils. The coloured pencils are complete!

THE ART PORTFOLIO

See the list of materials on page 48.

1 On the back of the rectangle of leatherette, draw two lines parallel to the short sides, 1.2cm (½in) from each edge.

2 Cut the piece of cardboard into two 7 × 9cm (2¾ × 3½in) rectangles. Place them on the back of the leatherette and align their long external sides with the drawn lines.

3 Fold the edges of the leatherette over the long edges of the pieces of cardboard and hold in place with the mini clothes pegs (**a, b**).

4 Sew around the art portfolio, 4mm (³⁄₁₆in) from the edge.

5 Fold the two leaves of the art portfolio together. Knot the elastic around the art portfolio to hold it closed (**c, d**).

The art portfolio is complete!

To download the pictures to slip into Loulou's art portfolio, visit www.bookmarkedhub.com

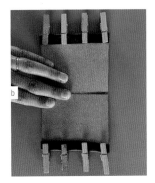

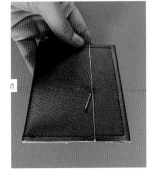

THE RABBIT HAT

See the list of materials on page 48.

CUTTING AND TRACING DIAGRAM

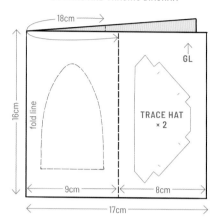

The hat

7 Trace the outline of the hat twice on the wrong side of the 16 × 8cm (6⁵⁄₁₆ × 3⅛in) pieces of faux fur and cut out. (This gives you the front and back.)

8 Cut the following from the piece of double-sided fusible interfacing:
• 4 strips measuring 4.8 (1⅞in) × 7mm (¼in)
• 2 hat edges

9 On the wrong side of the front and back of the hat, iron on these four strips of interfacing at the positions shown in green on the pattern (see page 87). In the same way, iron the hat edges cut from the interfacing in the positions shown in green on the pattern.

10 Remove the protective backing from the pieces of double-sided fusible interfacing.

11 Overcast all the edges of the front and back of the hat.

12 Position the ears on the front of the hat, right sides together, following the markings on the pattern. The base of the ears should stick out 5mm (³⁄₁₆in) from the edges of the hat. Sew along the base of the ears, 1cm (⅜in) from the edge (**c**).

13 Fold each interfaced part of the front and back of the hat wrong sides together (**d**). Protect the faux fur with a cloth and press the folded parts with an iron (**e**).

14 Cut the piece of single-sided fusible interfacing into two strips measuring 4 × 1.3cm (1½ × ½in). Place on the wrong side, at the base of the ears. Protect the faux fur with a cloth and press with an iron. Remove the protective backing: the base of each ear is now secured against the wrong side of the hat (**f**, **g**).

15 Place the front and back of the hat right sides together. Sew along the top of the hat between the ears, 7mm (¼in) from the edge.

16 Sew along the edges of the hat as shown in pictures **h** and **i**, 1cm (⅜in) from each corner, forming a perpendicular line of stitches at the bottom of the hat. Turn the hat the right way out.

Your rabbit hat is complete! Pop the hat on your cat's head (**j**) and pull its ears out through the two concealed gaps behind the rabbit ears (**k**).

1 Following the cutting diagram, cut the faux fur into three pieces:
• 1 piece 16 × 18cm (6¼ × 7in) for the ears
• 2 pieces 16 × 8cm (6¼ × 3in) for the front and back of the hat.

The ears

2 Trace the outline of the ear twice on the wrong side of the rectangle of peach cotton, leaving a space of at least 1cm (⅜in) outside the traced lines, except at the base of the ears.

3 Place this fabric on the rectangle of faux fur of the same size, right sides together. Sew around the lines, leaving the base of the ears open.

4 Cut around the ears, 5mm (³⁄₁₆in) from the seams and directly against the openings.

5 Turn the ears the right way out, making sure you push out the points. At the base of each ear fold the sides to the middle, inside to inside (so cotton against cotton).

6 Sew along the base of the ears, 5mm (³⁄₁₆in) from the edge, to hold the folds in place (**a**). Set to one side for now.

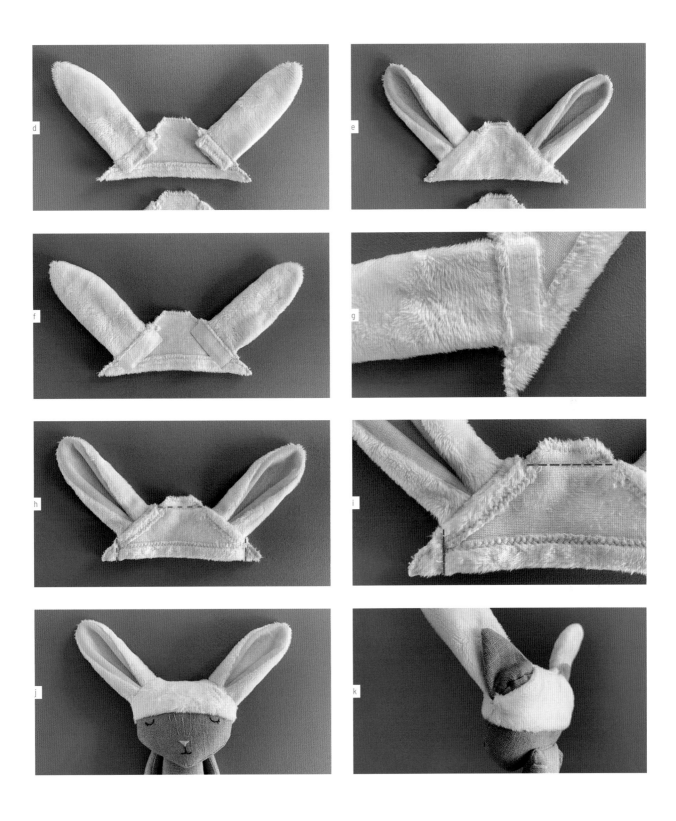

COCO

~~~

Coco loves science, especially meteorology. She loves sunshine and storms alike.

THE MIDI-SKIRT

See the list of materials on page 48.

1 Overcast all edges of the fabric rectangle.

2 Fold the rectangle in half widthways and sew the two shorter edges together, 5mm (³⁄₁₆in) from the edge. Press the seam open with an iron.

3 Turn under 1cm (³⁄₈in) along one long side and stitch 7mm (¼in) from the edge to make the hem for the elasticated waist. Ensure you leave a 2cm (¾in) gap open.

4 Turn under 6mm (¼in) along the second long edge and sew 4mm (³⁄₁₆in) from the edge to hem the skirt.

5 Thread the elastic into the hem using a safety pin.

6 Turn the skirt the right way out.

7 Adjust to the cat's waist size by pulling gently on the ends of the elastic. Knot the ends of the elastic and cut off the excess.

8 Sew up the gap in the waistband with slip stitch. The skirt is complete! (**a**)

THE BOOTS

See the list of materials on page 48.

1 Fold one of the rectangles in half lengthways, right sides together. Pin the long side edges together to hold them in place.

2 Place the boot pattern on the rectangle, the dotted lines on the pattern along the fabric fold and the top of the pattern against the top of the rectangle. Trace the outline of the boot (**a**).

3 Sew round the line and cut out the boot, leaving a 4mm (³⁄₁₆in) seam allowance.

4 Turn the boot the right way out and make the second boot in the same way (**b**). The boots are complete!

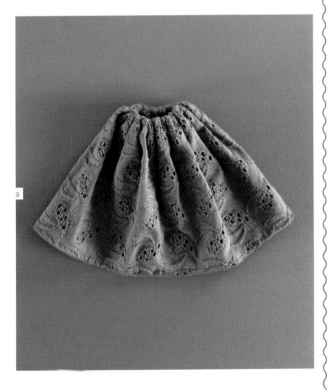

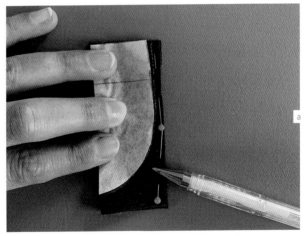

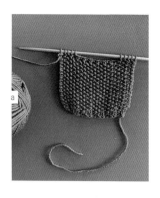

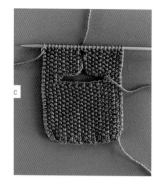
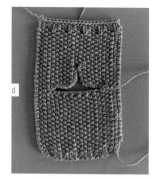

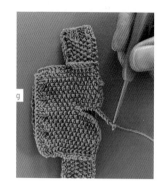

THE RETRO JUMPER

See the list of materials on page 48 and the basic knitting instructions on pages 25–31.

The retro jumper is worked in two parts:
- the front and the back of the body, knitted in a single piece
- the arms, knitted directly on to the body after picking up some stitches.

The body

1 The body is worked from the bottom of the front.
Cast on 22 sts.
Rows 1 and 2: work in k2 p2 rib.
Rows 3 to 28: continue in seed stitch (k1 p1). Even rows knit first stitch, odd rows purl first stitch.
Row 29: work 5 sts in seed stitch, cast off (bind off) 12 sts for neckhole, work remaining 5 sts in seed stitch: the work is separated into two (**a**).
2 Rows 30 to 32: only work the 5 sts on the LH side of the jumper.
Row 33: cable cast on 7 sts (see technique on page 30): you now have 12 sts. Work these 7 new sts in seed stitch starting with p1. K2tog and work last 3 sts in seed stitch: you have 11 sts.
Rows 34 to 42: work these 11 sts in seed stitch (**b**).

3 Cut the yarn, leaving a tail of approximately 30cm (11¾in). Leave this side for now. Do not turn the work over.
4 Return to the second side of row 30.
Rows 30 and 31: work these 5 sts in seed stitch.
Row 32: cable cast on 7 sts. You now have 12 sts.
Work these 7 new sts in seed stitch starting with k1. P2tog and continue last 3 sts in seed stitch: you now have 11 sts.
Rows 33 to 40: work these 11 sts in seed stitch.
Row 41: work the first 11 sts, then the 11 sts set aside previously: the two sides rejoin and the neckline slit is formed (**c**).
Rows 42 to 56: work rows without further shaping.
Rows 57 to 58: work in k2 p2 rib.
Row 59: cast off (bind off) all sts (**d**).

The sleeves

5 On the RH side of the body, pick up 16 sts along the armhole: start 2.5cm (1in) from the bottom of the front of the top and finish 2.5cm (1in) from the bottom of the back of the top (**e**) (for more details, see Picking up stitches at the edges on page 30).

6 Rows 1 to 11: work rows in seed stitch without further shaping. Rows 12 to 13: work in k2 p2 rib then cast off (bind off) 16 sts (**f**).

7 Work the second sleeve on the LH side of the body, following the instructions in steps 5 and 6.

Assembling and finishing

8 Fold the jumper, right sides together. By hand, use the working yarn to sew the sides and the undersides of the sleeves together in backstitch.

9 Work in the end of the yarn located at the bottom of the neckhole slit, up one side of the slit. Do not cut off the tail of yarn.

10 Fasten off all the other tails and snip off any excess.

11 Using the tail at the top of the slit, crochet 7 ch to make a button loop (**g**). Insert the hook next to the slit, a few millimetres below the start of the chain to form a loop (**h**). Fasten off with 1 sl st and work in the end of the yarn.

12 Turn the jumper the right way out. Sew the little button on the other side of the slit, opposite the button loop.

The retro jumper is complete (**i**)! Put it on over the cat's feet, before putting on the skirt.

THE BOW HEADBAND

See the list of materials on page 50.

See the list of materials on page 50.

CUTTING DIAGRAM

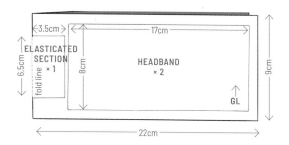

1 Cut three rectangles from the piece of fabric, following the instructions on the cutting diagram (the headband pieces measure 8 × 17cm/3¼ × 6¾in) and the elasticated part 6.5 × 7cm (2½ × 2¾in).

2 Overcast the edges of all the pieces.

The headband

3 On the wrong side of each headband piece, insert a pin to mark a point on one of the long sides that is 7cm (2¾in) from the edge, and a second marking 4cm (1⁹⁄₁₆in) from the first. These mark the position of the gap.

4 Fold one of the headband pieces in half lengthways, right sides together.

5 Sew along one of the short ends, then along one of the long sides, 5mm (³⁄₁₆in) from the edge. Leave the gap open.

6 Remove the pins and clip the corners on the short edge.

7 Repeat for the second headband piece and set to one side for now (**a**).

Elasticated section

8 Fold the rectangle of the elasticated section in half lengthways, right sides together. Sew along the long sides, 5mm (³⁄₁₆in) from the edge, to form a tube.

9 Turn the tube the right way out and position the seam at the back.

10 Thread the elastic through the tube so it sticks out 1cm (³⁄₈in) from the entrance. Centre it on the tube's width. Secure the start of the elastic by sewing across the open end of the tube, 5mm (³⁄₁₆in) from the edge (**a**).

11 Pull on the elastic so 1cm (³⁄₈in) sticks out from the other end of the tube. Centre it on the tube's width. Secure the end of the elastic by sewing across the open end of the tube, 5mm (³⁄₁₆in) from the edge (**b**).

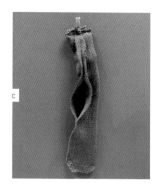

Assembling

12 Insert the elasticated section into the open end of one of the headband pieces. Align the seam along the length of the elasticated section with the seam along the long side of the headband piece.

13 Allow 1cm (⅜in) of fabric (elasticated section) to stick out from the end of the headband piece. Sew across the short end, 7mm (¼in) from the edge (**c**).

14 Turn the headband piece the right way out through the gap and turn out the elasticated section and all corners of the headband.

15 Insert this headband piece and the elasticated section into the second headband piece through the gap in the long side. Align the seam along the length of the elasticated section with the seam of the long side of the headband piece (**d**).

16 Allow 1cm (⅜in) of fabric (elasticated section) to stick out from the end of the second headband piece and sew along this short end, 7mm (¼in) from the edge (**d**).

17 Bring out the first headband piece and the elasticated section through the gap in the second headband piece and turn it the right way out (**e**).

18 Turn under 5mm (³⁄₁₆in) from the edges of the gaps in the two headband pieces and sew up using slip stitch (**f**).

19 Adjust the length of the headband around your cat's head, positioning the elasticated section at the back. Use a double knot to tie the two headband pieces together (**g**).

The headband is complete! The elasticated section means you do not have to undo the knot when you want to put it on or take it off your cat.

JEANNE

Jeanne is a baker.
She is as greedy as she is
chatty, and loves to serve
up cakes and the latest
gossip for all her friends.

THE SHAWL

See the list of materials on page 50 and the basic knitting instructions on pages 25–31.
The instructions marked 🐱 are just for Jeanne and the ones marked 🐱 just for Mina.

1 Cast on 🐱 3 sts/🐱 4 sts.
Row 1: work row in knit stitch.
Row 2: from here, continue in garter stitch, working 1 inc 🐱 at the start of each row, 2 sts from the edge until you reach 50 sts. Then continue with an inc at the start and end of each row, 2 sts from the edge/🐱 at the start and end of each row, 2 sts from the start and end of each row.
2 When you have reached 🐱 70 sts/🐱 50 sts, cast off (bind off) loosely enough to ensure some give.
Mina's shawl is complete!

🐱 For Jeanne:

3 Cut out a 5 × 2.5cm (2 × 1in) rectangle from the stiff cardboard.

4 Wrap the navy blue embroidery thread around the width of the cardboard pattern. Wrap round twelve times then cut the thread.

5 Holding all the loops of thread in place, pass an embroidery needle threaded with navy blue embroidery thread between the loops and the cardboard.

6 Place this thread at the end of the loops of thread, along one of the long edges of the cardboard (**a**). Tie a tight double knot, gathering all the loops of thread together.

7 Cut the loops of thread on the other edge of the cardboard to release the tassel (**b**).

8 Wrap the bronze embroidery thread round the top of the tassel (the part where the strands are knotted together). Wind it round twice then tie a double knot (**c**). Snip off the ends of the bronze thread.

9 Trim the strands to the same length with scissors to form an attractive tassel (**d**).

10 Make two other tassels in the same way and sew them to each corner of the shawl.

Jeanne's shawl is complete! (**e**)

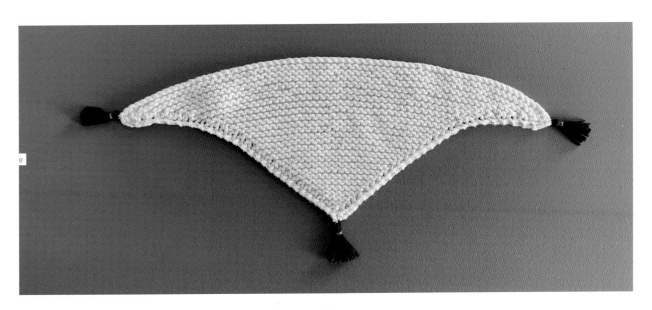

THE SWEETHEART-NECKLINE DRESS

See the list of materials on page 50.

CUTTING DIAGRAM

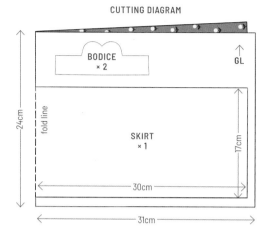

1 Cut out the three pattern pieces for the dress, following the instructions in the section Making fabric clothes on page 8.

The bodice

2 Overcast the long side along the bottom of the two bodice pieces.

3 Place the two bodice pieces right sides together. Sew around the whole piece, other than the long side that you overcast previously (red line), 3mm (⅛in) from the edge.

4 Turn the bodice the right way out, pushing out the corners carefully.

5 Place the bodice on the paper pattern and use a pin to mark A, A', B and B'. These mark the position of the shoulder straps.

Assembling the bodice and shoulder straps

6 Thread a tapestry needle with one of the pieces of elastic. Insert the needle at marking A, between two stitches on the hem, from the outside of the bodice to the inside. Pull the elastic gently between the two layers of fabric, leaving a short length of elastic outside the bodice.

7 Inside the bodice, tie a double knot in the end of the elastic and pull on it from outside the bodice as far as the knot will allow.

8 Insert a pin through the elastic, 3cm (1¼in) from the knot (which marks the start of the strap) (**a**).

9 Thread the needle with the elastic again and insert it at mark A', between two stitches on the hem, from the outside of the bodice to the inside, as far as the pin will allow (**a**).

10 Inside the bodice, tie a double knot in the end of the elastic, so the pin is held against mark A'. Cut off any excess elastic.

11 Repeat the steps given above for the second shoulder strap, using marks B and B' (**b, c, d**).

12 Turn under 5mm (³⁄₁₆in) from the edges of the bottom of the bodice and press with an iron. Set to one side for now.

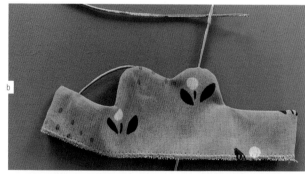

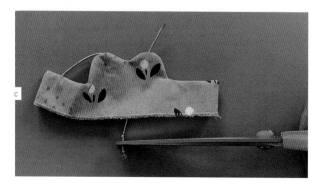

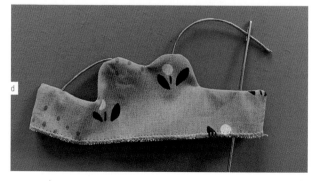

The skirt

13 Overcast the edges of the rectangle of the skirt, except for one of the long sides: this will be the bottom of the skirt.

14 Using straight stitch, sew a row of gathers along the long, overcast side, 5mm (³⁄₁₆in) from the edge (see Making a row of gathers on page 13). Sew a second line of gathers, parallel to the first, 1cm (⅜in) from the edge.

15 Pull gently on the gathering stitches to reduce the width of the skirt to that of the bottom of the bodice plus 1cm (⅜in).

16 Knot the gathering threads in pairs and cut off the excess thread.

Assembling the skirt and bodice

17 Insert a small amount of toy filling in the two rounded sections of the bodice neckline.

18 Turn under 5mm (³⁄₁₆in) along the short edges of the skirt and press with an iron.

19 Insert the gathered side of the skirt into the gap in the bodice: all the gathers should be hidden within the bodice. Pin to hold in place (**e**).

20 Tack (baste) together by hand, near the bottom of the bodice: align the edges of the front and back of the bodice carefully in relation to the edges of the skirt (**f**, **g**).

21 Sew along the bottom of the bodice, just over the tacking (basting) stitches, then pull out the tacking (basting) thread.

Finishing touches

22 Turn the dress wrong side out. Align the back short sides of the dress, right sides together, and sew them together, 3mm (⅛in) from the edge, starting 2cm (¾in) beneath the bodice. Press the seam open with an iron.

23 Overcast the bottom of the dress.

24 Turn under 7mm (¼in) along the bottom of the dress and sew along the fold, 5mm (³⁄₁₆in) from the edge.

25 Turn the dress the right way out. Sew the two halves of the small snap fastener to the back, 5mm (³⁄₁₆in) from the edge of each side of the bodice (**h**).

The sweetheart-neckline dress is complete! Pull on the dress over the cat's feet.

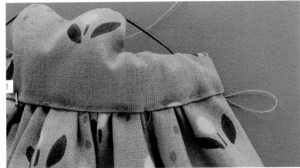

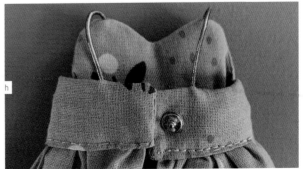

THE LACY TIGHTS

See the list of materials on page 50.

1 Stick the pieces of self-adhesive soluble fabric stabilizer to the wrong side of the pieces of lace, then place the two pieces of lace right sides together.

2 Centre the pattern on the lace and pin together to hold in place (**a**). Cut around the pattern to make two legs (**b**).

3 Use a pencil to mark a small line at O and O' on the stabilizer side.

4 Overcast the top of the legs and the two back crotch lines with markings O and O'.

5 Place the two legs right sides together and sew up the front crotch line using zigzag stitch.

6 Open out the legs and turn under 1cm (⅜in) along the top of the legs. Sew along the fold in straight stitch, 7mm (¼in) from the edge, to make the hem for the elasticated waist.

7 Thread the elastic into the waist hem. Pull on the ends of the elastic to adjust it to the size of the cat's waist.

8 Knot the ends of the elastic and cut off any excess. Slip the knot into the waistband.

9 Place the two legs right sides together. Straight stitch along the back crotch line, 4mm (³⁄₁₆in) from the edge, leaving the gap O–O' free (**c**).

10 Place the front and back of the tights right sides together, aligning the middle of the front with the middle of the back. Sew round the inner legs using zigzag stitch (**d**).

11 Immerse the tights in a little warm water and rub gently until the fabric stabilizer has completely dissolved. Slip them between two layers of towelling (terrycloth) and press to absorb any excess water. Leave flat to dry.

12 Once dry, turn the right way out. The tights are complete!

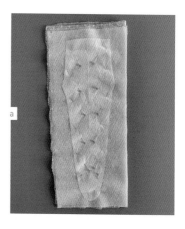

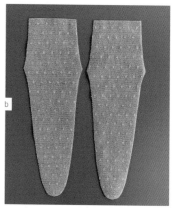

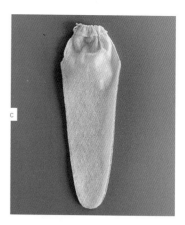

THE POINTY HAT

See the list of what you need on page 50.
The instructions marked 🐱 are for Jeanne,
🐱 for Marcel and 🐰 for the hares.

1 Trace the hat pattern on to the wrong side of the chosen fabric and cut out. Use a pointed pencil to transfer markings R and R' to the wrong side of the fabric (see technique on page 33).

2 Fold the hat right sides together so the two straight sides are aligned. Sew the straight sides together, 3mm (⅛in) from the edge. Clip the corners at the ends (**a**).

3 Turn the hat the right way out.

4 🐱🐰 Use the fork to make a pompom, 3cm (1¼in) in diameter, following steps 1 to 5 on page 84.

5 Stick the pompom on top of the hat with a glue gun.

6 Make a little loop at the end of the elastic thread and tie a knot.

7 Insert the thick, pointed needle through mark R, from the inside of the hat and pull the thread as far as the knot will allow. Insert the needle at mark R', from the outside of the hat, and pull the thread through (**b**).

8 Measure 🐱 14cm (5½in)/ 🐱 19.5cm (7½in)/ 🐰 11cm (4¼in) of thread from the initial knot and make another little loop at this second end. Tie a knot (**c**).

The pointy hat is complete! (**d**)

For **Jeanne** and **Marcel**, pull the hat on like a necklace, then lift it and place it on the top of the head.

For **the hares**, place the hat on the head: the elastic goes under the chin, in front of one ear and behind the other.

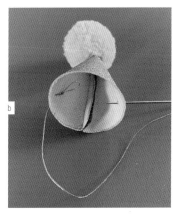

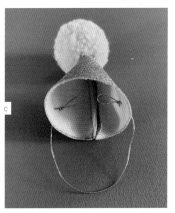

BILLIE

~~~

Billie has green fingers.
She is very sensitive.
It is Billie who gave the club its
name after hearing Coco explain
how rainbows are formed.

THE ANKLE BOOTS

See the list of what you need on page 50.

1 Fold one of the squares of leatherette in half, right sides together. Pin the long side edges together to hold them in place.

2 Place the boot pattern on the square, the dotted line on the pattern along the fabric fold and the top of the pattern against the top of the square. Trace the outline of the boot.

3 Use the point of a pencil to transfer mark F. Cut the slit down the fold as far as mark F (**a**).

4 Sew round the line and cut round the boot, leaving a 4mm (³⁄₁₆in) seam allowance (**b**).

5 Turn the boot the right way out.

6 Using the long needle, pierce two holes either side of the slit. Thread through the elastic to make an X-shaped lace, using pictures **c** and **d** as reference.

7 Knot the ends of the elastic inside the boot and cut off the excess.

8 Make the second boot in the same way.

The boots are complete!

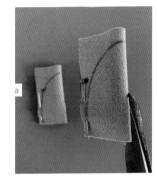
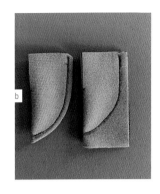

THE LEAF HEADBAND

See the list of what you need on page 50.

1 Trace and cut out from the felt the large leaf shape four times and the small leaf twice.

2 Put a dab of hot glue in the centre of the base of each leaf at the mark shown on the patterns.

3 Fold the leaves inwards towards the dab of glue at the base and pinch until the glue holds.

4 Thread the needle with the elastic and insert through the back of each leaf at the fold. Bring the needle back out, 5mm (³⁄₁₆in) from where it went in. Sew two large leaves and one small leaf in one direction, then one small and two large in the other. Knot the ends of the thread together.

The leaf headband is complete! Place it around the cat's head, positioning three leaves to the right of her head and three leaves to the left.

THE POMPOM SCARF

See the list of what you need on page 50 and the basic knitting instructions on page 25.

1 Cast on 12 sts in pine green. Work in stocking (stockinette) stitch for 54cm (21¼in). Cast off (bind off) the 12 sts.

2 Fold one end in half, right side of knit to right side and sew along this short end with slip stitch, using the tail of yarn (**a**). Do the same for the other end. Work in the ends of the yarn.

3 Make two pompoms in the ecru yarn, following steps 1 to 5 on page 84.

4 Using doubled sewing thread, sew a pompom to each end of the scarf (**b**).

The scarf is complete!

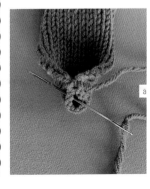

THE HALTERNECK DRESS

See the list of what you need on page 50.

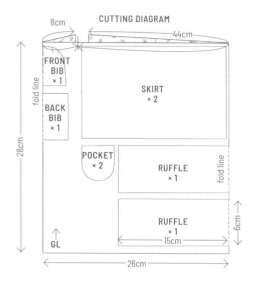

CUTTING DIAGRAM

8cm

44cm

FRONT BIB × 1

BACK BIB × 1

SKIRT × 2

POCKET × 2

RUFFLE × 1

RUFFLE × 1
15cm

28cm

26cm

fold line

fold line

GL

6cm

The halterneck dress is made in two parts: the bib and the skirt.

The bib

1 Cut out the eight pattern pieces for the dress, following the instructions in the section Making fabric clothes on page 8. The ruffles measure 30 × 6cm (11¾ × 2½in).

2 Place the front and back of the bib right sides together (the back bib piece is bigger than the front bib piece to facilitate sewing the hem on fine fabric). Insert the two pieces of ribbon between the two pieces of fabric at the marks shown on the front bib pattern piece. Pin to hold in place.

3 Sew around the bib, 4mm (³⁄₁₆in) from the edge, leaving the straight edge along the bottom (red line) open. Trim off the excess fabric from the rectangle (**a**) and turn the bib the right way out.

4 Overcast the bottom of the bib, sewing through both layers of fabric together. Set to one side for now (**b**).

The front of the skirt and the pockets

5 Overcast all round the edges of the pocket pieces.

6 Turn under 5mm (³⁄₁₆in) along the top of each pocket and sew along the top of the pocket, 3mm (⅛in) from the edge (**b**).

7 Using the sewing thread, tack (baste) a row of gathers around the curved edges of the pocket (excluding the top edge), right up against the overcasting that you sewed previously (**c**). Do not tie a knot at the start or end of the sewing.

8 Cut out the small pocket pattern piece from the cardboard.

9 Place the cardboard pattern piece on the wrong side of one of the tacked (basted) pockets. Align the top edge of the pocket and the top of the pattern piece.

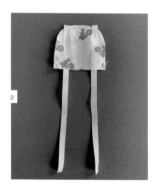
a

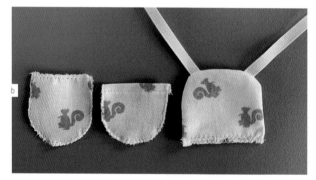
b

c

d

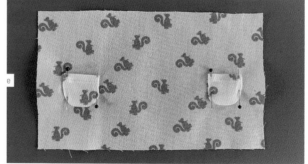
e

10 Pull gently on the ends of the gathering thread, ensuring the cardboard pattern remains in place: the edges of the pocket fold round the pattern piece and take on its curved shape (**d**).

11 Press with an iron to hold the edges in place. Remove the cardboard and the gathering thread.

12 Position the pocket on the front of the skirt, wrong side against right side, in accordance with the marking shown on the pattern, and pin to hold in place.

13 Sew around the pocket (except for the top edge), 2mm (¹⁄₁₆in) from the edge.

14 Repeat from step 9 for the second pocket (**e**).

The front of the skirt and the bib

15 Overcast the edges of the skirt.

16 Sew a row of gathers along the top edge of the skirt, 5mm (³⁄₁₆in) from the edge (see Making a row of gathers, page 13). Sew a second line of gathers parallel to the first, 8mm (⁵⁄₁₆in) from the edge (**f**).

17 At the top of the skirt, insert a pin at each of marks A, B and C (**f**).

18 At the bottom of the bib, insert a pin to mark the middle.

19 Place the bib and the front of the skirt right sides together, aligning the bottom edge of the bib with the top edge of the skirt. Align the middle of the bib with mark B on the skirt. Pin together (**g**).

20 Align marks A and C with the edges of the bib. Pin together.

21 Pull gently on the gathering stitches to reduce the width of the skirt between marks A and C to the width of the bottom of the bib (**h**, **i**).

22 Arrange the gathers attractively between A and C. Sew between A and C, 1cm (³⁄₈in) from the edge (**j**) through both layers of fabric.

23 Remove the gathering threads and set to one side for now.

The back of the skirt

24 Overcast all edges of the back of the skirt.

25 Turn under 1cm (³⁄₈in) at the top of the skirt. Sew along the fold, 8mm (⁵⁄₁₆in) from the edge to make the hem for the elasticated waist.

26 Using a safety pin, thread the elastic through the waistband. Secure the start of the elastic in place by putting in a line of stitches 3mm (¹⁄₈in) from the edge. Sew backwards and forwards a couple of times to ensure the seam is secure (**k**).

27 Reduce the length of the elasticated waistband to 5cm (2in) (**l**). Secure the end of the elastic in place by putting in a line of stitches 3mm (¹⁄₈in) from the edge. Sew backwards and forwards a couple of times to ensure the seam is secure.

28 Snip off the excess elastic and set to one side for now.

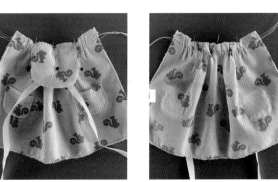

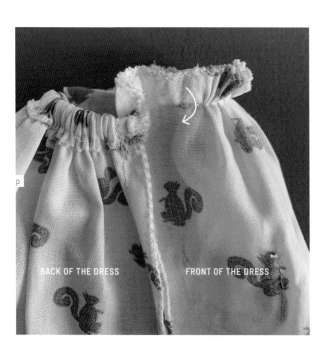

BACK OF THE DRESS   FRONT OF THE DRESS

The ruffles, the front and back of the skirt

29 Overcast all edges of the ruffles.

30 Sew a line of gathers along one of the long sides of each ruffle, 5mm (3⁄16in) from the edge: this will be the top of the ruffle. Sew a second line of gathers parallel to the first, 8mm (5⁄16in) from the edge.

31 Divide the top of each ruffle into four equal parts and put in three pins to mark these points (**m**).

32 Divide the bottom of the front and back of the skirt into four equal parts and put in three pins to mark these points. Set one of the ruffles and the front of the skirt to one side for now.

33 Place the second ruffle on the back of the skirt, right sides together, aligning the edges of the pinned sides.

34 Align the markings on each piece and pin together (**n**).

35 Pull gently on the gathering stitches: distribute the gathers evenly, reducing the width of the ruffle to that of the bottom of the skirt. Pin all along to make it easier to sew the two pieces together (**o**).

36 Sew along the bottom of the skirt, 1cm (3⁄8in) from the edge, then remove the pins and gathering stitches.

37 Press the seam allowances towards the top of the skirt with an iron.

38 Topstitch 3mm (1⁄8in) from the seam to hold the seam allowances against the wrong side of the skirt.

39 Do the same with the ruffle and the front of the skirt, repeating from step 34.

Assembling the front and back of the dress

40 Place the front and back of the dress right sides together, keeping the bib folded downwards. Align the bottom edges of the dress: the top of the skirt front should extend 1cm (3⁄8in) beyond the top of the skirt back.

41 Pin the sides of the dress and sew up the sides, 5mm (3⁄16in) from the edge: start at the bottom of the ruffle and sew to the top of the elastic waistband of the back. Press the seam allowances towards the front of the skirt with an iron.

42 On the front of the skirt, fold the ends of the top edges down against themselves, so as to hide the start and end of the elastic (**p**).

43 Hold in place with a few hand stitches on either side (**q**).

44 Bring the bib out through the waist opening. Fold the bottom of the bib against the inside of the skirt (**r**). Hand sew each side of the bottom of the bib to the top of the folded skirt with a few stitches (**s**).

45 Turn under 5mm (3⁄16in) along the bottom of each ruffle. Sew along the fold, 3mm (1⁄8in) from the edge to make the hem. Turn the dress the right way out.

The halterneck dress is complete!

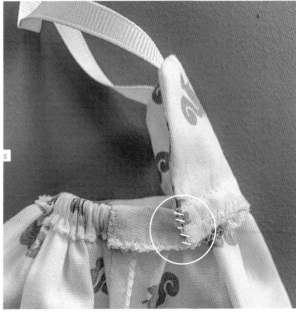

OLIVIA

Olivia is always happy and full of energy. Her babysitting services are much in demand as she loves inventing games and stories for the children she looks after.

THE SNAP-FASTENED CARDIGAN

See the list of materials on page 50 and the basic knitting instructions on pages 25-31.

The back

1 Cast on 22 sts.
Rows 1–4: work in k2 p2 rib.
Rows 5–20: continue in stocking (stockinette) stitch.
Rows 21–24: continue in stocking (stockinette) stitch with 2 dec at the start of each row, to form the armholes. 14 sts remain.
Rows 25–31: continue in stocking (stockinette) stitch.
Row 32: cast off (bind off) 14 sts.
Set the back to one side for now.

The RH front half

2 Cast on 12 sts.
Rows 1–4: work in k2 p2 rib.
Rows 5–19: continue in stocking (stockinette) stitch.
Row 20: continue in stocking (stockinette) stitch with 2 dec at the start of the row to form the armhole. 10 sts remain.
Row 21: work the 10 sts in stocking (stockinette) stitch.
Row 22: continue in stocking (stockinette) stitch with 2 dec at the start of the row. 8 sts remain.
Rows 23–24: continue in stocking (stockinette) stitch.
Row 25: continue in stocking (stockinette) stitch with 3 dec at the start of the row to form the neckhole. 5 sts remain.
Rows 26–29: continue in stocking (stockinette) stitch.
Row 30: cast off (bind off) the 5 sts.
Set the RH front half to one side for now.

The LH front half

3 Cast on 12 sts.
Rows 1–19: repeat as for the RH front half.
Row 20: continue in stocking (stockinette) stitch.
Row 21: continue in stocking (stockinette) stitch with 2 dec at the start of the row to form the armhole. 10 sts remain.
Row 22: work the 10 sts in stocking (stockinette) stitch.
Row 23: continue in stocking (stockinette) stitch with 2 dec at the start of the row. 8 sts remain.
Rows 24–25: continue in stocking (stockinette) stitch.
Row 26: continue in stocking (stockinette) stitch with 3 dec at the start of the row to form the neckhole. 5 sts remain.
Rows 27–29: continue in stocking (stockinette) stitch.
Row 30: cast off (bind off) the 5 sts. Set the LH front half to one side for now.

The sleeves

4 Cast on 14 sts.
Rows 1–4: work in k2 p2 rib.
Row 5: continue in stocking (stockinette) stitch, making 1 inc on each side. You have 16 sts.
Rows 6–11: continue to *work stocking (stockinette) stitch for 5 rows then 1 inc on first and last sts of next row*. You have 18 sts.

Rows 12–23: repeat twice more from * to *. You have 22 sts.
Rows 24–25: work rows in stocking (stockinette) stitch without further shaping.
Rows 26–29: continue in stocking (stockinette) stitch with 2 dec at the start of the row. 14 sts remain.
Row 30: continue in stocking (stockinette) stitch.
Row 31: cast off (bind off) the 14 sts.
5 Work a second identical sleeve.

Assembling and finishing

6 To sew up the shoulders, place each half front piece on the back of the cardigan, right sides together. By hand, use backstitch to sew them together, threading a thick darning needle with the working yarn.

7 To sew on the sleeves, align the armholes of the sleeves and body, right sides together. Sew the sleeves to the arm holes using backstitch.

8 Sew the undersides of the arms together then the sides of the body, right sides together, using backstitch.

9 Fasten off and clip tails.

10 Sew on a snap-fastener at the bottom of the cardigan to do it up (a).

The cardigan is complete!

THE DUNGAREES

See the list of what you need on page 50.

The dungarees are made in two parts: the trousers and the bib.

1 Cut out the four pattern pieces for the dungarees, following the instructions on page 8 for Making fabric clothes.

CUTTING DIAGRAM

GL

TROUSERS
× 2

fold line

27cm

BIB
× 2

12cm

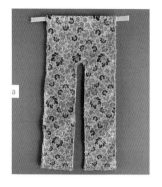

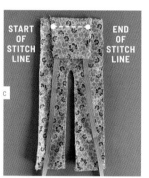

START
OF
STITCH
LINE

END
OF
STITCH
LINE

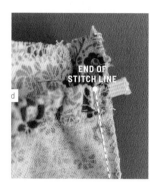

END OF
STITCH LINE

The trousers

2 Overcast the edges of the front and back of the trousers using zigzag stitch. Set the front of the trousers to one side for now.

3 At the top of the back of the trousers, fold under 1cm (⅜in), wrong sides together. Sew 5mm (³⁄₁₆in) from the edge to form the waistband.

4 Insert the flat elastic into the waistband, allowing its ends to stick out on either side.

5 Sew across one end of the waistband, 2mm (¹⁄₁₆in) from the edge, to close it and secure the elastic in place. Go backwards and forwards to ensure the stitching is very secure (**a**).

6 Pull on the other, unstitched end of the elastic, to reduce the width of the waistband to 5cm (2in). Sew across the unstitched end of the waistband, 2mm (¹⁄₁₆in) from the edge, to close it and secure the elastic in place. Go backwards and forwards to ensure the stitching is very secure. Snip off the excess elastic and set the back of the trousers to one side for now (**b**).

The bib

7 Place the front and back of the bib right sides together. Insert the two pieces of ribbon between the two pieces of fabric at the marks shown on the pattern. The ends of the ribbons should stick out 5mm (³⁄₁₆in) from the top of the bib. Pin the ribbons to hold them in place.

8 Sew around the bib, 4mm (³⁄₁₆in) from the edge, leaving the straight edge along the bottom (red line) open.

9 Turn the bib the right way out, pushing the corners out carefully. Overcast the bottom of the bib in zigzag stitch, sewing through both layers of fabric together.

Assembling the bib and the front of the trousers

10 Place the bib on the front of the trousers, right sides together, aligning the bottom edge of the bib with the top edge of the trousers. Centre the bib in accordance with the markings.

11 Sew along the bottom of the bib, 1cm (⅜in) from the edge (**c**). Leave the bib on the front of the trousers, right sides together, ribbons downwards.

Assembling the trousers

12 Place the back of the trousers on the front, right sides together (the bib is still downwards). Line up the edges of the bottom of the legs: the stitch line of the bib and the front of the trousers should extend 1cm (⅜in) beyond the top of the back of the trousers.

13 Sew along the two sides of the legs, 3mm (⅛in) from the edge: from the bottom of the legs up to the elastic waist of the back of the trousers (**d**).

14 Open out the seams. Turn under 1cm (⅜in), wrong sides together, at the bottom of each trouser leg. Sew 7mm (¼in) from the fold, to form the hems.

15 Sew around the crotch, 4mm (³⁄₁₆in) from the edge, right sides together.

16 Turn the dungarees the right way out. Leave the bib downwards against the front of the trousers: fold the sides of the front top of the trousers against themselves, wrong sides together (**e**).

17 Sew them into place in this position with a few hand stitches. Bring the bib the right way up: the bottom of the bib swings inside the trousers, positioned against the seam allowance of the waistband (**f**, **g**).

18 Hand sew each side of the bottom of the bib to the waistband of the trousers (**h**).

The dungarees are complete! Knot the straps behind Olivia's neck with a little bow (**i**).

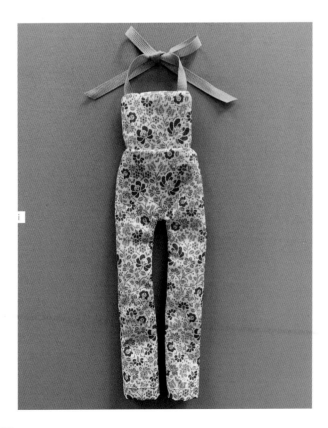

THE POMPOM HEADBAND

See the list of what you need on page 50.

1 Thread a needle with wool without tying a knot in the end. Set to one side for now.

2 Take the fork and wrap the wool from the ball around the prongs, staying in the middle of the fork. Keep hold of the end of the wool with the hand holding the fork. Wind around 60–70 times, depending on the thickness of your wool (**a**, **b**).

3 Holding the loops carefully in place, pass the needle threaded with the wool between the middle tines of the fork. Wrap it around the loops of wool and pull tight (**c**). Wrap it around the pompom again then knot tightly (**d**). Cut off any excess wool.

4 Slide the pompom off the fork (**e**).

5 Slip one blade of the scissors through the loops and snip through them all (**f**). Trim the strands to the same length to create an attractive ball (**g**, **h**).

6 Use a needle to thread the elastic through the centre of the pompom. Adjust it around the cat's head. Knot the ends of the elastic together and cut off the excess.

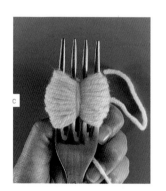
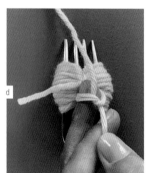

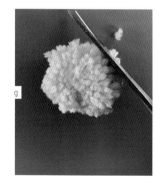

THE TOTE BAG

See the list of materials on page 50 and the basic crocheting instructions on pages 16–24.

1 Start with the bag, which is crocheted in the round. Make an adjustable ring.
Round 1: 6 dc in the adjustable ring (= 6 sts).
Round 2: 1 inc in each st (= 12 sts).
Round 3: 1 dc in each st (= 12 sts).
Round 4: *1 dc, 1 inc*, repeat 5 more times from * to * (= 18 sts).
Round 5: 1 dc in each st (= 18 sts).
Round 6: *2 dc, 1 inc*, repeat 5 more times from * to * (= 24 sts).
Round 7: 1 dc in each st (= 24 sts).
Round 8: *3 dc, 1 inc*, repeat 5 times from * to * (= 30 sts).
Rounds 9–13: 1 dc in each st (= 30 sts).
Round 14: *3 dc, 1 dec*, repeat 5 more times from * to * (= 24 sts).
Round 15: 1 dc in each st (= 24 sts).
2 Continue by crocheting in rows to form the shoulder strap.
*1 ch st, then 1 dc in each of next 2 sts. Flip work over.
* Rep from * to * another 35 times.
3 You have reached the end of the shoulder strap. Finish the work with 1 sl st, leaving a sufficient length of thread to sew the end of the strap to the bag, opposite its starting point.
4 Fasten off and clip tails.
5 Using a darning needle, thread the ribbon through one side of the tote and bring it back out a stitch further on. Tie a bow. The tote is complete!

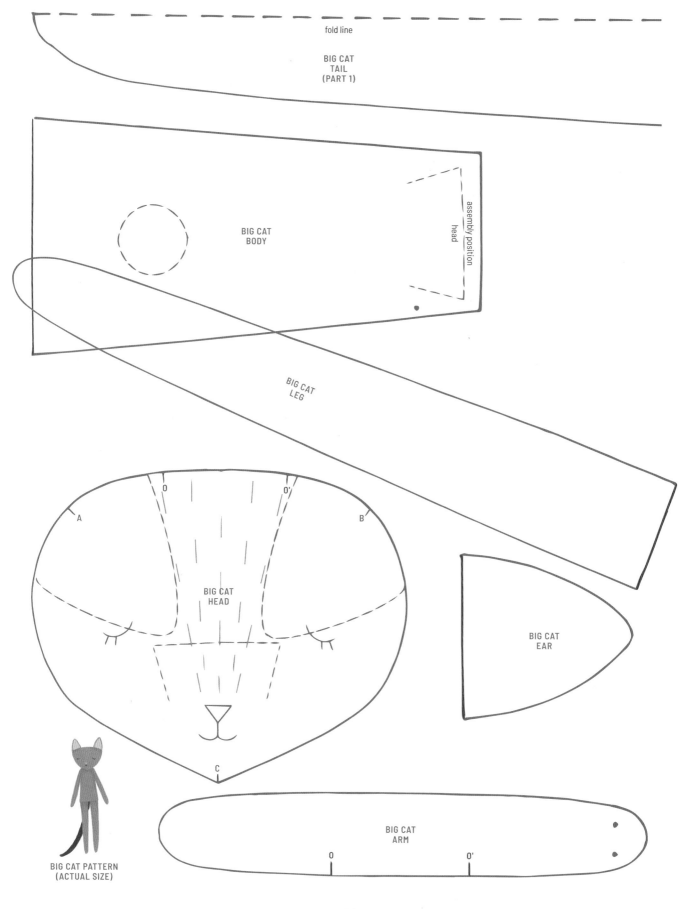

fold line

BIG CAT
TAIL
(PART 1)

BIG CAT
BODY

assembly position
head

BIG CAT
LEG

A

O   O'

B

BIG CAT
HEAD

BIG CAT
EAR

C

BIG CAT PATTERN
(ACTUAL SIZE)

BIG CAT
ARM

O   O'

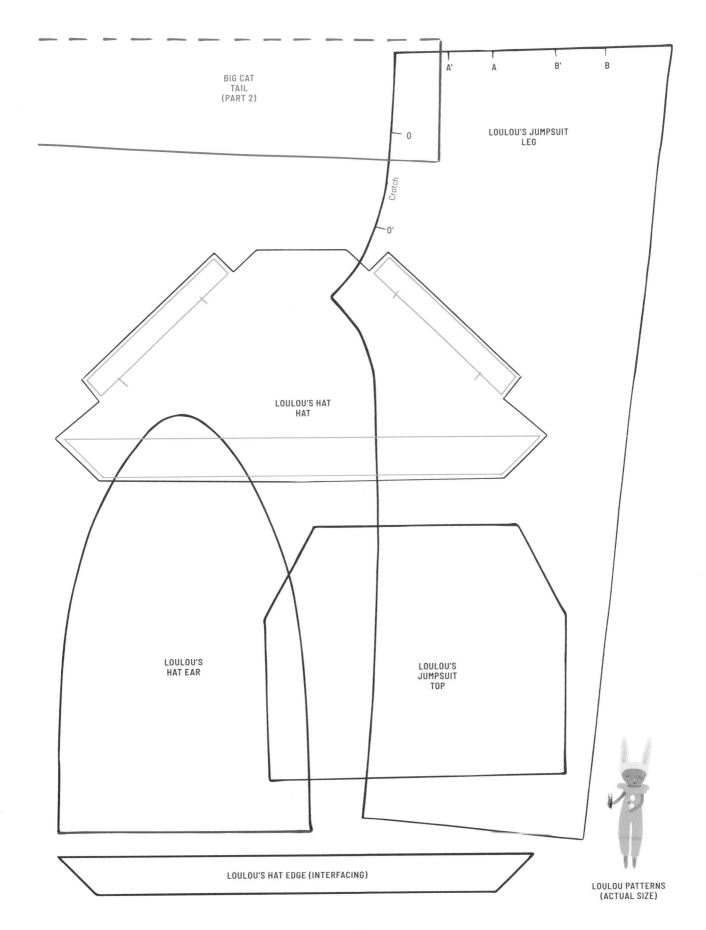

BIG CAT
TAIL
(PART 2)

A' A B' B

LOULOU'S JUMPSUIT
LEG

0

Crotch

0'

LOULOU'S HAT
HAT

LOULOU'S
HAT EAR

LOULOU'S
JUMPSUIT
TOP

LOULOU'S HAT EDGE (INTERFACING)

LOULOU PATTERNS
(ACTUAL SIZE)

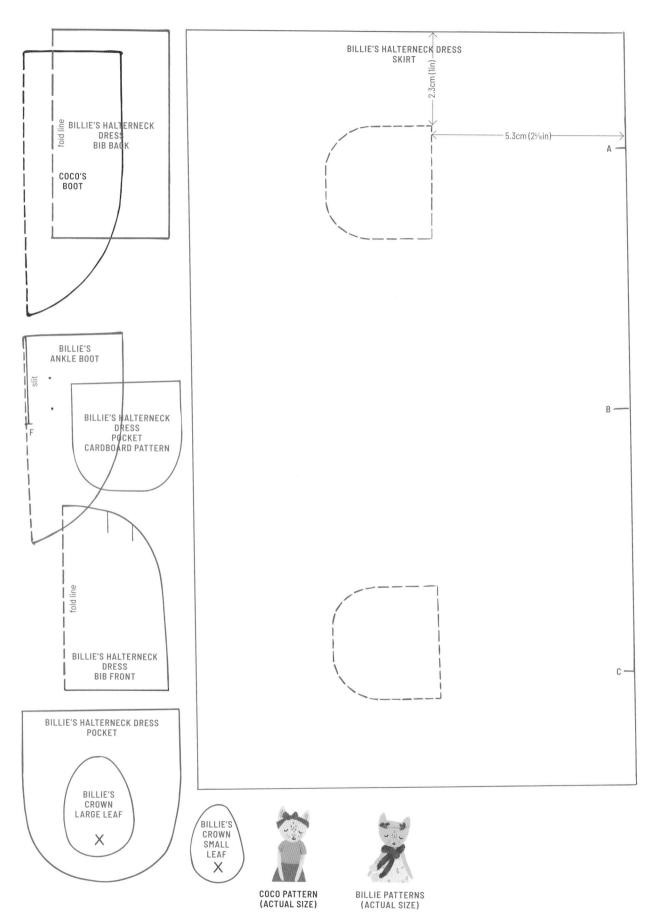

BILLIE'S HALTERNECK DRESS
BIB BACK

fold line

COCO'S
BOOT

BILLIE'S HALTERNECK DRESS
SKIRT

2.3cm (1in)

5.3cm (2¹⁄₁₆in)

A

BILLIE'S
ANKLE BOOT

slit

F

BILLIE'S HALTERNECK
DRESS
POCKET
CARDBOARD PATTERN

B

fold line

BILLIE'S HALTERNECK
DRESS
BIB FRONT

C

BILLIE'S HALTERNECK DRESS
POCKET

BILLIE'S
CROWN
LARGE LEAF

X

BILLIE'S
CROWN
SMALL
LEAF

X

COCO PATTERN
(ACTUAL SIZE)

BILLIE PATTERNS
(ACTUAL SIZE)

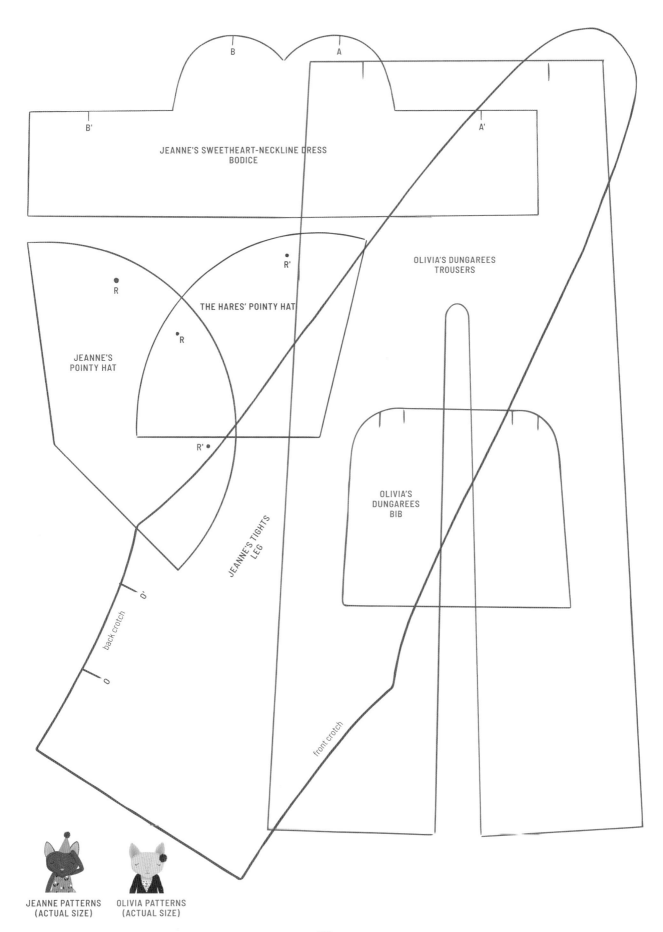

JEANNE'S SWEETHEART-NECKLINE DRESS
BODICE

B

A

B'

A'

OLIVIA'S DUNGAREES
TROUSERS

R'

THE HARES' POINTY HAT

R

JEANNE'S
POINTY HAT

R

R'

OLIVIA'S
DUNGAREES
BIB

JEANNE'S TIGHTS
LEG

O'

back crotch

O

front crotch

JEANNE PATTERNS
(ACTUAL SIZE)

OLIVIA PATTERNS
(ACTUAL SIZE)

Marcel the balancing bear

Finished size: 25cm (9¾in)
The patterns can be found on page 100.
For more details of the techniques used, see the Techniques section on page 10.

Marcel the bear
× 30 × 52cm (11¾ × 20½in) short pile faux fur in dark brown
× 2 chenille stems, 27cm (10¾in) long
× Sewing thread in brown and a colour to contrast with the fur
× DMC embroidery cotton in black
× 30cm (11¾in) cotton cordonnet crochet yarn, 0.3mm thick, in brown
× Toy filling
× Long pointed needle
× 4 pattern pieces (body, arm, ear, muzzle)

The pointy hat
× See the list of materials on page 50

The waistcoat
× 10.5 × 28cm (4¼ × 11in) velvet in red
× 10.5 × 28cm (4¼ × 11in) cotton poplin (or another fairly lightweight fabric such as cambric), in a colour to contrast with the red velvet
× Sewing thread to match chosen fabrics
× Sewing thread in yellow ochre
× Approximately 30cm (11¾in) shirring elastic in gold
× 2 buttons, Ø 7mm (¾in), in white
× 2 pattern pieces (front, back)

The pouch
× 7 × 10cm (2¾ × 4in) linen in teal
× 22 × 2cm (8½ × ¾in) linen in teal
× 7 × 10cm (2¾ × 4in) printed cotton (or poplin, cambric, polycotton or similar) in sea-green
× Sewing thread in teal and sea-green

The ball
× 20 × 10cm (7¾ × 4in) cotton in ecru
× 5-ply (sport) cotton knitting yarn, in bright yellow
× Toy filling
× 40g (1½oz) of stuffing pellets or rice
× Crochet 3mm (UK 11, US 2/3) hook
× Marker ring
× 1 pattern piece (counterweight)
× Stitches and techniques used: adjustable ring • double crochet (dc) • increase (inc) • decrease (dec)

Since Rustine cartwheeled her way into his heart, Marcel has rediscovered his balance.
He feels light and happy. It is lovely to see: they seem to move as one.

MARCEL THE BEAR

See the list of materials on page 90.

1 Following the cutting diagram, cut the faux fur into four pieces:
- 2 pieces 30 × 14cm (11¾ × 5½in) for the body
- 2 pieces 30 × 12cm (11¾ × 4¾in) for the muzzle, ears and arms.

The muzzle, arms and ears

2 On the wrong side of one of the pieces of 30 × 12cm (11¾ × 4¾in) faux fur, trace the following in accordance with the cutting diagram:
- the outline of the muzzle × 1
- the outline of the arms × 2
- the outline of the ears × 2.

Leave a space of at least 1cm (⅜in) around the lines. Transfer the position of gaps O–O' on the arms.

3 Place this piece of fabric on the second piece of the same size, right sides together, and sew each of the pieces along the lines marked, leaving open gaps O–O' on the arms, the base of the ears and the base of the muzzle (red lines).

4 Trim the pieces to 4mm (³⁄₁₆in) from the seams and the gaps and directly against the openings of the ears and muzzle.

5 Turn each piece the right way out and fill the muzzle with toy filling. Set the arms and muzzle to one side for now.

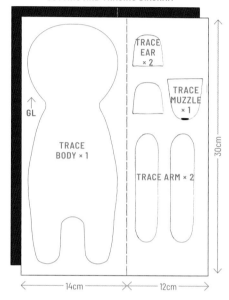

CUTTING AND TRACING DIAGRAM

TRACE EAR × 2

TRACE MUZZLE × 1

GL

TRACE BODY × 1

TRACE ARM × 2

30cm

14cm

12cm

Assembling the body and ears

6 On the wrong side of the pieces of 30 × 14cm (11¾ × 5½in) faux fur, trace the outline of the body, aligning parts 1 and 2 to form a single piece. Leave a space of at least 1cm (⅜in) around the line. Transfer the position of gap O–O' and markings A and B.

7 Transfer the position of the ears to the right side of the fabric. To do so, use a needle with double-thickness thread in a contrasting colour to sew by hand round the line of the head where the ears are positioned in running stitch. Do not oversew to start or finish. Form large stitches on the right side of the fabric and smaller ones on the wrong side: the outline of the head will then be clearly visible on the right side (**a**, **b**).

Next, sew a cross on the wrong side to mark the position of C. Do not oversew (**c**). Position the pattern piece on the right side of the fabric, aligning the outline of the head with the line, and mark C with the embroidered cross on the right side.

Place the ears on the pattern piece at the positions marked and pin the base of the ears to the fabric to hold them in place (**d**, **e**). Carefully remove the pattern piece: its work is done!

8 Place this piece of fabric on the second piece of the same size, right sides together. Pin the two layers together and sew round the outline of the body, leaving gap O–O' open.

9 Cut around the body, 4mm (³⁄₁₆in) from the seam and the gap.

10 Turn the body the right way out and stuff firmly. Pack more toy filling into the stomach to form a nice, rounded tummy.

11 Turn under 4mm (³⁄₁₆in) on either side of the gap and sew up using slip stitch.

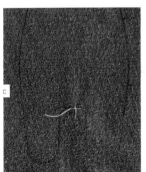

Sewing on the muzzle

12 Turn under 4mm (³⁄₁₆in) on either side of the muzzle opening.

13 Position the top of the muzzle 4cm (1⁹⁄₁₆in) from the top of the head. Sew it to the face with slip stitch, stitching through the fold in the muzzle and the face in turn. Sew all round the muzzle in the same way (**f**, **g**).

14 Split a length of embroidery cotton so you only have two strands. Using a single length of this thread, embroider the nose in satin stitch: start along the seam line, forming a horizontal stitch, 1cm (³⁄₈in) in length; then continuing with shorter and shorter stitches one underneath the other.

15 Using the same thread, embroider the eyes 1cm (³⁄₈in) either side of the muzzle and 1cm (³⁄₈in) above the seamline of the muzzle: embroider several French knots, one on top of the other.

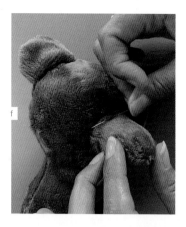

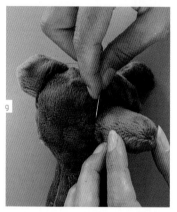

The arms

16 Fold one of the two pieces of chenille stem in half. Twist the two ends together for around 1cm (³⁄₈in). Bend this twisted section back against the rest of the chenille stem (**h**).

17 Place the piece of chenille stem inside the arm (**i**). Turn under 4mm (³⁄₁₆in) on either side of the gap. Sew up using slip stitch.

18 Do the same for the other arm.

Attaching the arms

19 Attach the arms to the body with cordonnet crochet yarn, following the instructions on page 32.

Your bear is complete!

THE POINTY HAT

See the list of materials on page 50.
The instructions for making the pointy hat are the same as those for Jeanne's hat on page 73.
Put the pointy hat on Marcel's head as shown in this picture.

THE WAISTCOAT

See the list of materials on page 90.

CUTTING DIAGRAM

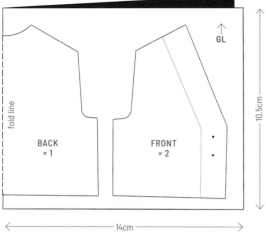

GL

fold line

BACK
× 1

FRONT
× 2

10.5cm

←————— 14cm —————→

In velvet for the outer fabric
In poplin for the lining

1 Cut out the three pattern pieces for the waistcoat, following the instructions in the section Making fabric clothes on page 8.

2 Set your sewing machine to the decorative stitch of your choice and do a few test runs first on an off-cut of velvet.

3 Using the yellow ochre thread, use this decorative stitch to sew all along the opening of the two front pieces, 1.5cm (½in) from the edge.

4 Place the two front pieces on the back of the velvet waistcoat, right sides together. Pin the shoulders edge to edge and sew along them with straight stitch, 4mm (³⁄₁₆in) from the edge. Press the seams open with an iron.

5 Do the same for the two poplin front pieces and the poplin back of the waistcoat.

6 Place the velvet waistcoat and the poplin lining right sides together. Pin around the armholes to keep the two layers of fabric together. Likewise pin around the neckline and the front pieces. Sew along the armholes, 4mm (³⁄₁₆in) from the edge. Sew around the front edges and the neckline, 4mm (³⁄₁₆in) from the edge (**a**).

7 Clip the curves and turn the waistcoat the right way out (**b**).

8 Align the sides of the waistcoat, right sides together, then as an extension of this seam, the sides of the lining. Pin (**c**). Sew along the sides, 4mm (³⁄₁₆in) from the edge (**d**). Press the seams open with an iron (**e**).

9 Align the bottom of the waistcoat with the bottom of the lining, right sides together. Sew along the bottom of the waistcoat, 4mm (³⁄₁₆in) from the edge. Leave gap O–O' open (**f**).

10 Turn the right way out, ensuring you push out the corners nicely.

11 Turn under 4mm (³⁄₁₆in) on either side of the gap and sew up using slip stitch.

Finishing touches

12 Sew the two buttons to the front of one of the sides of the waistcoat, between the embroidery and the edge, spaced 1cm (³⁄₈in) apart.

13 On the other side, immediately opposite the buttons, insert a needle threaded with elastic through the seam between the lining and the waistcoat. Bring the needle back out 2mm (¹⁄₁₆in) further along the seam. Leave a 1cm (³⁄₈in) length of elastic and knot the two ends together. Snip off the excess.

The waistcoat is complete!

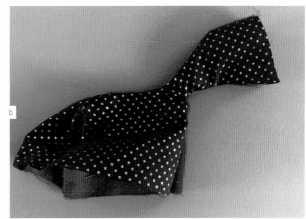

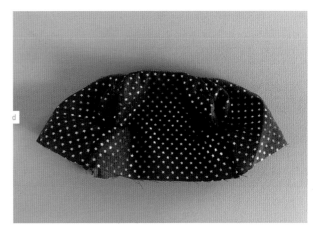

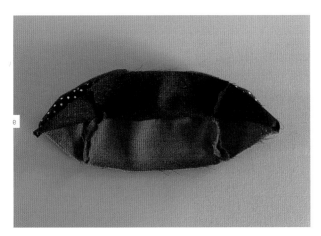

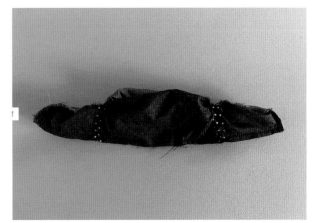

THE POUCH

See the list of materials on page 90.

The lining

1 Cut the piece of cotton into two 5 × 7cm (2 × 2¾in) rectangles.

2 On one of the pieces, mark a 4.5cm (1¾in) gap along the middle of one of the long sides of the rectangle.

3 Place the two lining pieces right sides together. Sew round the lining, 3mm (⅛in) from the edge, leaving one long side (the top of the bag) and the gap open.

4 Clip the corners and set to one side for now.

The shoulder strap

5 Fold the 22 × 2cm (8½ × ¾in) band in half lengthways, wrong sides together. Mark the fold in the middle with an iron, then open out.

6 Fold each side inwards, wrong sides together, to the centre fold (**a**). Fold one side over the other along the central fold (**b**).

7 Sew along the open edge, 1mm (⅟₁₆in) from the edge.

The outside of the bag

8 Cut the piece of linen into two 5 × 7cm (2 × 2¾in) rectangles.

9 Place the two pieces right sides together. Sew round the bag 3mm (⅛in) from the edge, leaving one long side (the top of the bag) open.

10 Clip the corners and turn the bag the right way out.

11 Position the ends of the shoulder strap on either side of the bag, against the seam between the two sides. Centre the width of the strap on the seam. Allow the ends of the strap to extend 5mm (³⁄₁₆in) above the top of the bag (**c**).

12 Secure the ends of the strap to the bag with a few machine or hand stitches across the width of the strap, 3mm (⅛in) from the edge of the bag (**d**).

Assembling the bag

13 Tuck the bag inside the lining, which is still the wrong way out. Bring out the strap through the gap in the bottom of the lining so there are not too many layers.

14 Align the edge seams carefully, as well as the top edges of the bag and the lining. Sew around the top edge of the bag, 5mm (³⁄₁₆in) from the edge (**e**). Turn out the bag through the gap in the lining (**f**, **g**).

15 Turn under 3mm (⅛in) on either side of the gap. Sew up using slip stitch.

16 Push the lining back inside the bag (**h**).

The pouch is complete!

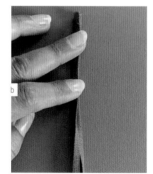
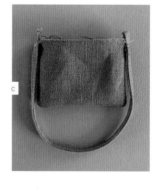

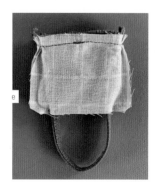

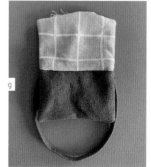

THE BALL

See the list of materials on page 90 and the basic crocheting instructions on pages 16–24.

The counterweight

1 Fold the piece of cotton in half widthways, right sides together. Cut into two squares.

2 On the wrong side of the pieces, trace the outline of the counterweight, leaving a space of at least 1cm (⅜in) outside the lines.

3 Place this fabric on the second piece of cotton, right sides together. Sew around the counterweight on the line, leaving a 4cm (1½in) gap.

4 Cut and notch around the counterweight, 4mm (³⁄₁₆in) from the seam and the gap. Turn the right way out.

5 Fill the counterweight with stuffing pellets or rice (**a**).

6 Turn under 4mm (³⁄₁₆in) on either side of the gap. Sew up on the machine 2mm (¹⁄₁₆in) from the edge. Set to one side for now.

The ball

7 Crochet the ball:
Round 1: make an adjustable ring, then 6 dc in the ring (= 6 sts).
Round 2: 1 inc in each st (= 12 sts).
Round 3: *1 dc, 1 inc*, repeat 5 more times from * to * (= 18 sts).
Round 4: *2 dc, 1 inc*, repeat 5 more times from * to * (= 24 sts).
Round 5: *3 dc, 1 inc*, repeat 5 times from * to * (= 30 sts).
Round 6: *4 dc, 1 inc*, repeat 5 more times from * to * (= 36 sts).
Round 7: *5 dc, 1 inc*, repeat 5 more times from * to * (= 42 sts).
Round 8: *6 dc, 1 inc*, repeat 5 more times from * to * (= 48 sts).

Round 9: *7 dc, 1 inc*, repeat 5 more times from * to * (= 54 sts).
Round 10: *8 dc, 1 inc*, repeat 5 more times from * to * (= 60 sts).
Round 11: *9 dc, 1 inc*, repeat 5 more times from * to * (= 66 sts).
Round 12: *10 dc, 1 inc*, repeat 5 more times from * to * (= 72 sts).
Round 13: *11 dc, 1 inc*, repeat 5 more times from * to * (= 78 sts).
Round 14: *12 dc, 1 inc*, repeat 5 more times from * to * (= 84 sts).
Rounds 15–25: 1 dc in each st (= 84 sts).
Round 26: *12 dc, 1 dec*, repeat 5 more times from * to * (= 78 sts).
Round 27: *11 dc, 1 dec*, repeat 5 more times from * to * (= 72 sts).
Round 28: *10 dc, 1 dec*, repeat 5 more times from * to * (= 66 sts).
Round 29: *9 dc, 1 dec*, repeat 5 more times from * to * (= 60 sts).
Round 30: *8 dc, 1 dec*, repeat 5 more times from * to * (= 54 sts).
Round 31: *7 dc, 1 dec*, repeat 5 more times from * to * (= 48 sts).
Round 32: *6 dc, 1 dec*, repeat 5 more times from * to * (= 42 sts).

8 Fill the ball firmly with the toy filling. Insert the counterweight in the ball, on top of the toy filling (**b**, **c**).

9 Continue crocheting:
Round 33: *5 dc, 1 dec*, repeat 5 more times from * to * (= 36 sts).
Round 34: *4 dc, 1 dec*, repeat 5 more times from * to * (= 30 sts).
Round 35: *3 dc, 1 dec*, repeat 5 more times from * to * (= 24 sts).
Round 36: *2 dc, 1 dec*, repeat 5 more times from * to * (= 18 sts).
Round 37: *1 dc, 1 dec*, repeat 5 more times from * to * (= 12 sts).
Round 38: 6 dec (= 6 sts).

10 Using the darning needle, thread the yarn through the 6 remaining stitches and pull tight. Knot, and work in the end of the yarn (**d**).
The ball is complete!

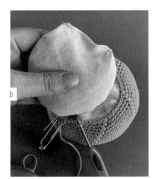
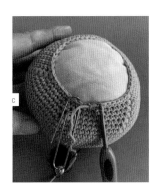

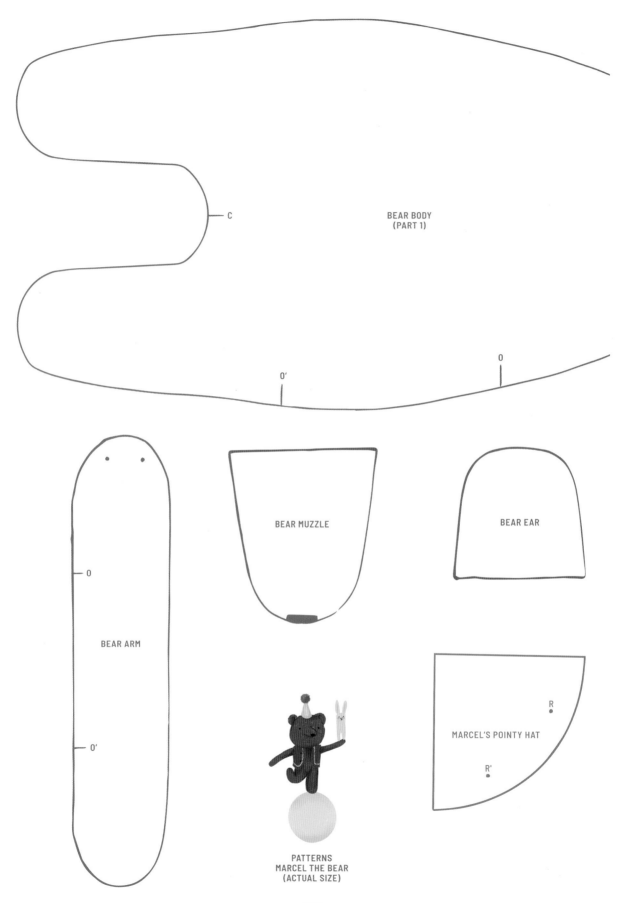

BEAR BODY
(PART 1)

C

O'

O

BEAR MUZZLE

BEAR EAR

O

BEAR ARM

O'

MARCEL'S POINTY HAT

R

R'

PATTERNS
MARCEL THE BEAR
(ACTUAL SIZE)

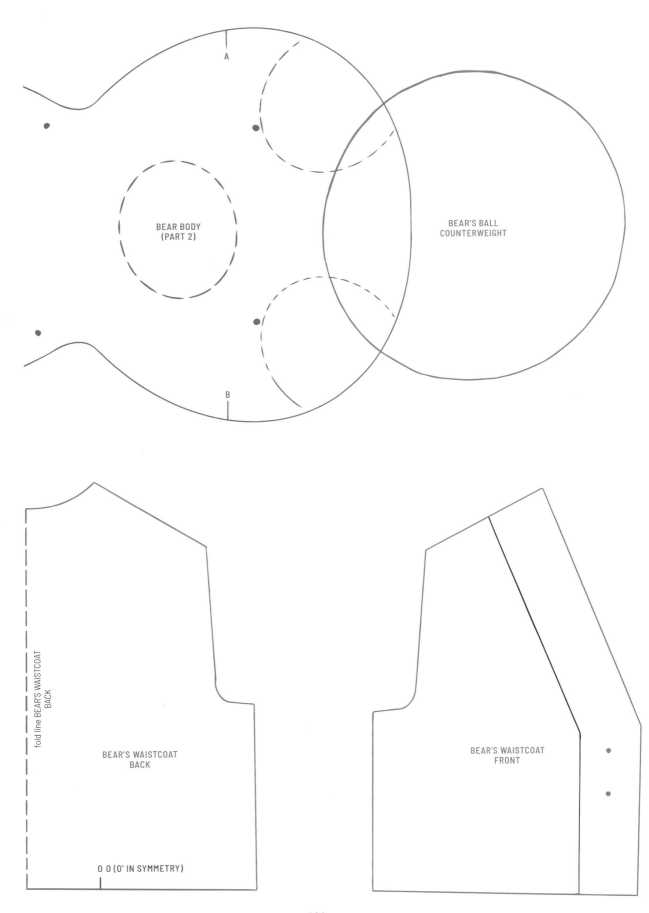

A

BEAR BODY
(PART 2)

BEAR'S BALL
COUNTERWEIGHT

B

fold line BEAR'S WAISTCOAT BACK

BEAR'S WAISTCOAT
BACK

0 0 (0' IN SYMMETRY)

BEAR'S WAISTCOAT
FRONT

The hot-air balloon cloud

MATERIALS

Finished size of mouse: 10cm (4in) • hot-air balloon cloud: 45cm (17¾in)
See page 111 for patterns.
For more details of the techniques used, see the Techniques section on page 10.

Lili the little mouse
× 13 × 22cm (5 × 8½in) cotton in light grey
× 4 × 6cm (1½ × 2½in) felt in pale pink
× Sewing thread in black and light grey
× Embroidery thread in metallic gold
× Toy filling
× 20cm (7¾in) cotton cordonnet crochet yarn, 0.3mm thick, in light grey
× 20cm (7¾in) cotton cordonnet crochet yarn, 0.3mm thick, in black
× Long pointed needle
× 3 pattern pieces (body, arm, ear)

The hot-air balloon cloud
× 44 × 33cm (17 × 13in) faux fur in off-white
× Sewing thread in ecru and bronze
× 3 lengths of embroidery thread in metallic gold, 50cm (20in)
× 5 lengths of 4, 5 or 8-ply (fingering, sport or DK) wool (each around 6m/6½yds), mix of colours
× 4, 5 or 8-ply (fingering, sport or DK) cotton crochet yarn, in bronze
× Nylon yarn
× Toy filling
× Crochet hook 3mm (UK 11, US 2/3)
× Marker ring
× Darning needle
× Long pointed needle
× Pins
× Fork
× Tape measure
× Mini clothes pegs
× 1 pattern (cloud)
× Stitches and techniques used: adjustable ring • double crochet (dc) • slip stitch (sl st) • increase (inc)

Go, because you want to.
Explore, learn and discover...
But promise us that you will return
one day to tell us about everything
that you have seen.

So Lili set off, taking all her dreams with her and remembered her promise.

LILI THE LITTLE MOUSE

See the list of materials on page 102.

1 Following the cutting diagram, cut the cotton into four pieces:
- 2 pieces 13 × 8cm (5 × 3¼in) for Lili's body
- 2 pieces 13 × 3cm (5 × 1¼in) for the arms.

CUTTING AND TRACING DIAGRAM

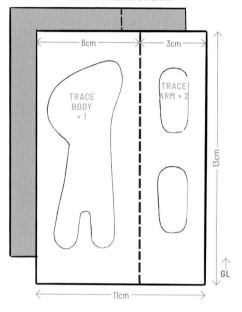

The ears

2 On the wrong side of the felt, trace and cut out the ear twice.

3 Fold the ear in half down the middle, right sides together. Sew together, by hand, the two sides A–B and A'–B, aligning A and A' (**a, b**). Set to one side for now.

The arms

4 On the wrong side of one of the pieces of 13 × 3cm (5 × 1¼in) faux fur, trace the outline of the arms twice, leaving a space of at least 1cm (⅜in) outside the lines. Mark the position of the gaps O–O'.

5 Place this piece of fabric on the second piece of the same size, right sides together. Sew round the arms along the line marked, leaving gaps O–O' open.

6 Cut around the arms, 4mm (³⁄₁₆in) from the seams and the gaps. Turn the arms the right way out and stuff lightly.

7 Turn under 4mm (³⁄₁₆in) from the edges of the gap. Sew up using slip stitch. Set the arms to one side for now.

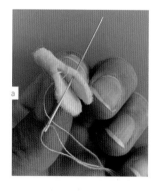

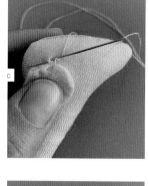
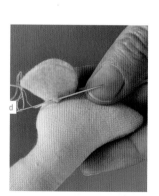
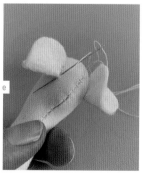
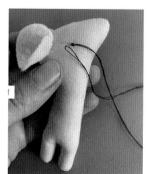
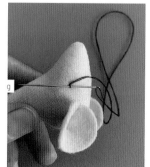
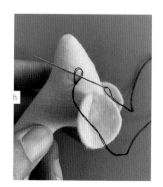

The body

8 On the wrong side of one of the pieces of 13 × 8cm (5 × 3¼in) cotton, trace the outline of the mouse's body, leaving a space of at least 1cm (⅜in) outside the lines. Mark the position of the gap O–O'.

9 Use a pin to transfer the position of the eye to the right side of the fabric (see technique on page 33). Use a pin to transfer the position of the ear to the right side of the fabric.

10 Place this piece of fabric on the second piece of the same size, right sides together. Sew round the body on the line marked, leaving the gap O–O' open.

11 Cut around your mouse, 4mm (³⁄₁₆in) from the seams and the gap.

12 Turn your mouse the right way out. Stuff firmly. Push the toy filling against the seams so the curves are nicely rounded.

13 Turn under 4mm (³⁄₁₆in) on either side of the gap and sew up using slip stitch.

Attaching the ears

14 Place the sewn side of the ear against the head, at the position marked. Sew the bottom of the ear to the head using slip stitch (**c**, **d**).

15 Sew the second ear to the other side of the head (**e**).

Finishing touches

16 Using doubled black thread, embroider a French knot for the eyes.

17 Then insert the needle at the base of the eye and push it through the head and out the other side to embroider the other eye (**f**, **g**, **h**).

18 Fasten off the thread and snip off the excess.

19 Using the doubled black thread, embroider the nose on the end of the muzzle using satin stitch (**i**).

20 Finish by passing the needle under all the stitches and snipping off the excess (**j**).

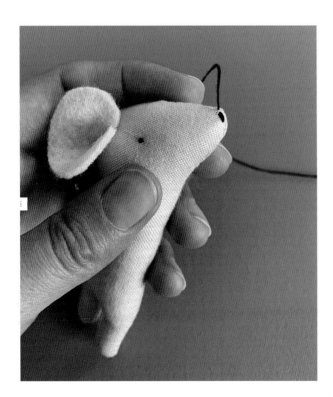

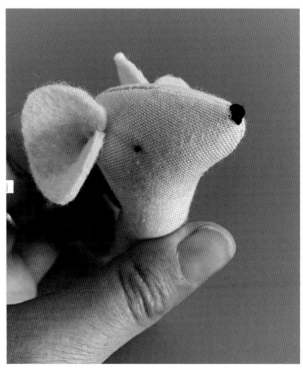

21 For the whiskers, use a doubled gold thread, knotting it 2cm (¾in) from the end.

22 Insert the needle in the cheek, between the eye and the neck and bring it out on the other side of the head, at the same level. Pull gently on the thread as far as the knot will allow.

23 Sew a small stitch on the other side of the head, just below the second whisker and tie a knot. Cut the second whisker, 2cm (¾in) from the cheek (**k**).

24 For the tail, use a needle threaded with single black cordonnet crochet yarn, knotting it at the end. Trim against the knot.

25 Insert the needle in the side of the body, between two seam stitches and bring it out on the mouse's back, 1cm (⅜in) from the top of the legs. Pull gently on the thread to pull the knot into the mouse's body.

26 Sew a small stitch at the base of the tail and tie a knot. Cut the cordonnet crochet yarn to the required length for the tail (**l**).

27 Attach the arms to the body with the grey cordonnet crochet yarn, following the instructions on page 32.

The little mouse is complete!

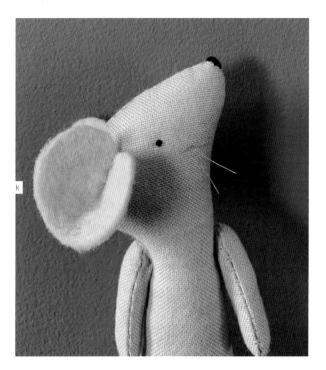

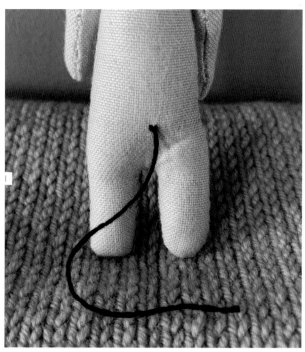

THE HOT-AIR BALLOON CLOUD

See the list of materials on page 102.

CUTTING AND TRACING DIAGRAM

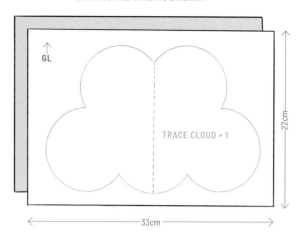

GL

TRACE CLOUD × 1

22cm

33cm

The cloud

1 Cut the faux fur into two 22 × 33cm pieces (8½ × 13in).

2 On the wrong side of the two pieces, trace the outline of half of the cloud, leaving a space of at least 1cm (⅜in) outside the line. Trace the other half of the cloud in symmetry.

3 Transfer marking O and mark O' symmetrically: these mark the position of the gap.

4 Place this piece of fabric on the second piece, right sides together. Sew round the cloud on the line marked, leaving the gap O–O' open. Sew backwards and forwards a few times at the start and end of the seam to ensure the ends of the gap are secure.

5 Cut around the cloud, 5mm (³⁄₁₆in) from the seam and the gap (**a**).

6 Turn the cloud the right way out and stuff firmly.

7 Turn under 5mm (³⁄₁₆in) on either side of the gap. Sew up using slip stitch.

The cloud is complete!

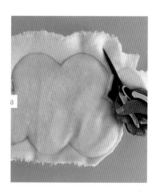

The basket

8 The basket is worked in the round.

Round 1: make an adjustable ring. Work 6 dc in this circle (= 6 sts).

Round 2: 1 inc in each st (= 12 sts).

Round 3: *1 dc, 1 inc*, repeat 5 more times from * to * (= 18 sts).

Round 4: *2 dc, 1 inc*, repeat 5 more times from * to * (= 24 sts).

Round 5: *3 dc, 1 inc*, repeat 5 times from * to * (= 30 sts).

Round 6: *4 dc, 1 inc*, repeat 5 more times from * to * (= 36 sts).

Round 7: *5 dc, 1 inc*, repeat 5 more times from * to * (= 42 sts).

Rounds 8–11: work 1 dc in each of the 42 sts, only working in the back loop of the sts of the previous round: this will form the stripes (= 42 sts) (**b**).

Rounds 12–17: work 1 dc in each of the 42 st, putting the hook normally under both loops of the sts of the previous round (= 42 sts) (**c, d**). At the end of round 17, finish the work with a sl st.

9 Work in the end of the yarn.

The pompoms

10 Use the fork to make five differently coloured pompoms, following steps 1 to 5 on page 84.

11 Insert a pin every 3.5cm (1½in) round the edge of the last round of the basket (**e**).

12 Sew a pompom at each spot marked by a pin, on the outside of the basket (**f** to **h**).

The basket is complete!

Assembling the hot-air balloon

13 Use a pin to mark F and F' on the front of the cloud and G on the back of the cloud, following the markings on the pattern and taking measurements on the cloud from the seam line.

14 Measure round the basket and divide this length into three so you can put in three pins, an equal distance apart (**i**).

15 Thread the long, pointed needle with an initial gold thread and tie a triple knot in the end.

16 Insert the needle in the seam of the cloud and bring it out at one of the markings (**j**) Pull the thread through as far as the knot will allow: the knot is hidden in the thickness of the cloud's fluff.

17 Do the same for the other two threads.

18 Place the mini clothes peg on one of the threads, 24cm (9½in) from where it comes out of the cloud (**k**).

19 Thread the end into the needle and insert it through one of the marks on the basket, under the last round, from outside to inside (**l**).

Pay close attention to which thread goes where: the thread from the back of the cloud goes to the marking on the back of the basket, for example. Pull the thread through as far as the mini clothes peg will allow (**m**). Knot to the basket with a double knot.

20 Do the same for the other two threads.

21 Bring the three tails of thread together and tie them in a simple knot under the basket, in the centre (**n**, **o**). You might prefer to snip off the gold threads, 2mm (¹⁄₁₆in) from each double knot.

22 Thread the needle with the nylon thread and tie a triple knot in the end.

23 Insert the needle in the back of the cloud, at mark H shown on the pattern. Bring the needle out through the seam at H'. Pull on the thread as far as the knot will allow.

24 Knot a loop at the other end of the nylon.

The hot-air balloon is finished and ready to be hung!

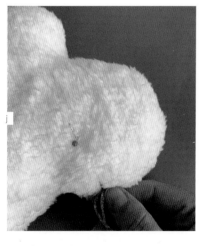

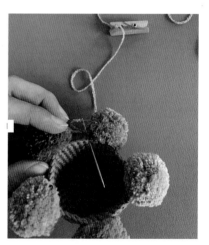

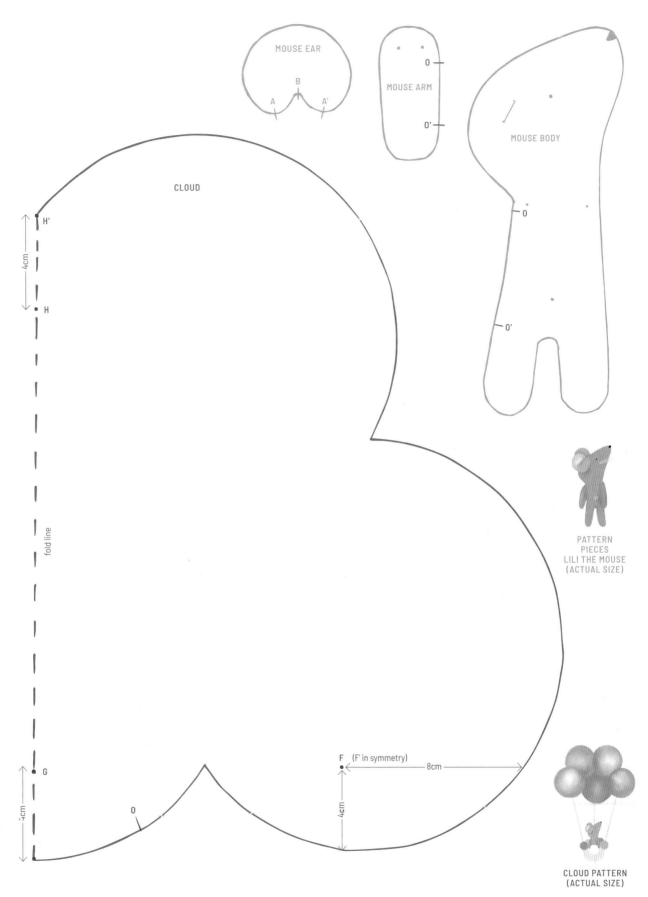

MOUSE EAR

B

A   A'

MOUSE ARM

O

O'

MOUSE BODY

O

O

O'

CLOUD

4cm

H'

H

fold line

G

4cm

O

F   (F' in symmetry)

8cm

4cm

PATTERN
PIECES
LILI THE MOUSE
(ACTUAL SIZE)

CLOUD PATTERN
(ACTUAL SIZE)

Jack the majestic bird

MATERIALS

Finished size: 19cm (7½in) from head to feet • 26cm (10¼in) with the wings
See page 119 for patterns.
For more details of the techniques used, see the Techniques section on page 10.

Jack the bird
× 24 × 28cm (9½ × 11in) cotton in teal
× 24 × 22cm (9½ × 8½in) cotton in ecru
× 24 × 22cm (9½ × 8½in) faux fur in ecru
× Sewing thread in black and teal
× Embroidery thread in metallic gold
× Shirring elastic in gold
× Toy filling
× Some stuffing pellets or rice
× Textile paint in gold
× Small, fairly fine paintbrush
× 4 pattern pieces (body, wing, leg, tail)
× Long pointed needle

The golden crown
× 6 × 7cm (2½ × 2¾in) sparkly gold paper
× Embroidery thread in metallic gold
× Paper glue
× Pencil
× Scissors
× Glue gun
× Mini clothes pegs
× 1 pattern (crown)

Look: my oversized wings stop me from flying. So, I walk...

And these wings that fall about me are a royal cloak that I wear with pride.

Do you see? What makes me different, makes me unique!

JACK THE MAJESTIC BIRD

See the list of materials on page 112.

CUTTING AND TRACING DIAGRAM

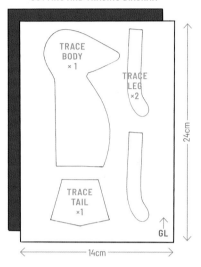

1 Cut the rectangle of teal cotton into two pieces, each measuring 24 × 14cm (9½ × 5½in).

2 On the wrong side of one of these pieces, trace the following with reference to the cutting diagram, leaving a space of at least 1cm (⅜in) between each piece:

- the outline of the body × 1
- the outline of the leg × 2
- the outline of the tail × 1

Use a pin to mark the position of the eye on the right side of the fabric (see technique on page 33).

3 Place this piece of fabric on the second piece of the same size, right sides together. Sew around the edge of each piece, following the line, leaving the openings marked with a red line open.

4 Cut around each piece, 3mm (⅛in) from the seams and directly against the openings. Clip the curves of the legs and turn each piece the right way out.

The head and the legs

5 Use a pin to transfer the position of the eye to the other side of the head.

6 Stuff the head, stopping at neck level. Push the toy filling hard up against the seams so the curves are nicely rounded.

7 Stuff the legs very firmly.

8 Use the gold paint to paint the beak (**a**) and the bottom of the legs (areas shown on the pattern pieces).

Ensure that the paint penetrates right into the seams. Leave to dry for an hour, then apply a second coat.

The tail

9 Reduce the width of the base of the tail to approximately 2.5cm (1in) by pushing the two sides in towards each other (**b, c**).

10 Sew along the opening, 4mm (³⁄₁₆in) from the edge to hold in place. Set to one side for now.

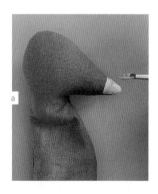

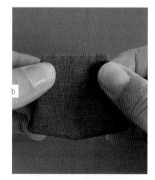

The wings

11 On the wrong side of the faux fur, trace the outline of the wing twice, leaving a space of at least 1cm (⅜in) outside the lines.

12 Place this fabric on the piece of ecru cotton, right sides together. Pin to hold the fabric in place (**d**).

13 Sew round the lines of the wings, leaving the base of the wings open (red line).

14 Cut around each wing, 5mm (³⁄₁₆in) from the seams and directly against the openings (**e**). Turn the wings the right way out.

15 Insert two teaspoons of stuffing pellets or rice in to each of the wings (**f**).

16 Turn under 5mm (³⁄₁₆in) on either side of the openings and sew up using slip stitch.

17 Position the pattern piece on top of each wing and insert a pin to indicate markings P–P' (**g**).

18 For the right wing, bring P to P', pinching together all the layers of fabric (**h**). To secure in place, stitch along the top edge of the wing, 8mm (⁵⁄₁₆in) from the edge.

19 For the left wing, do the reverse: bring P' to P then proceed as for the right wing. Set the wings to one side for now.

Assembling the bird

20 Tilt the bird's head forwards towards the front of the body. By hand, using a single teal sewing thread, secure the head in this position by sewing alternately under the chin (just in front of the beak) and the chest (in the seam line) (**i**, **j**). Oversew several times.

21 Finish stuffing the bird's body.

22 Turn under 5mm (³⁄₁₆in) on either side of the opening. Pinch the fold so the two seam lines are opposite each other (**k**).

23 Insert the tail in the gap and centre 1.5cm (½in) from either side of the opening (**l**).

24 Likewise insert one leg, in front of the tail, 5mm (³⁄₁₆in) from the side of the opening.

25 Sew up the opening, stitching alternately through the fold on each side, and through the leg and the tail (**m**, **n**). As you sew the opening closed, insert the second leg and finish the seam (**o**, **p**).

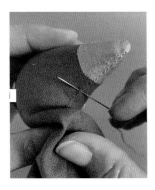

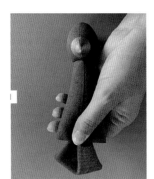
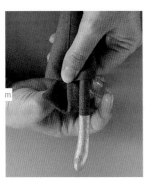
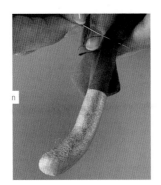

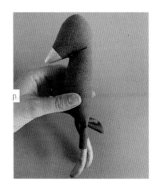

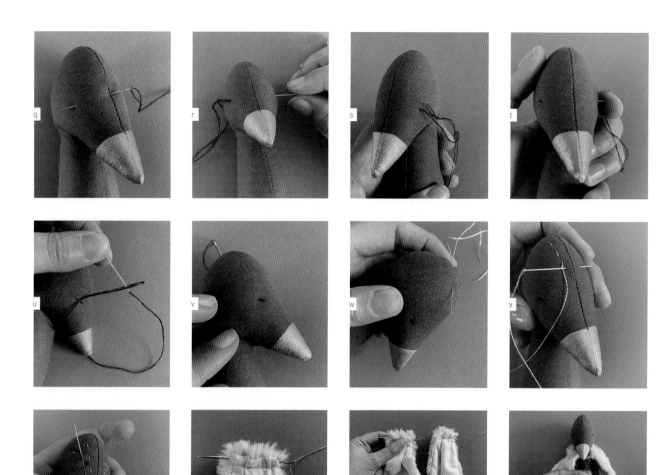

Finishing touches

26 Using doubled thread with a knot tied at the end, embroider the eyes: to do so, insert the needle in the seam of the head, between two stitches and bring it out at the position of the eye (**q**). Pull gently on the thread to pull the knot into the bird's head. Embroider a little 4mm (³⁄₁₆in) line. Bring the needle back out at the position of the second eye (**r**) and embroider another little 4mm (³⁄₁₆in) line (**s**). Bring the needle back out at the location of the first eye (**t**). Tie a knot and pull it into the head (**u, v**).

27 Using a single gold embroidery thread, embroider little lines in straight stitch on the top of the head (**w, x, y**). Likewise, embroider three small vertical V-shapes on either side of the stomach. Follow the steps given for embroidering the eyes to hide the knots at the start and end of the embroidery.

28 Thread a needle with shirring elastic, but do not tie a knot at end. Insert the needle at the top of one wing, between the two layers of fabric. Bring it out on the other side of the wing (**z**). Do the same with the second wing (**a**).

29 Adjust the length of the elastic around the bird's neck and knot the two ends together (**b**). Slide the wings to the correct position on either side of the bird's body.

The majestic bird is complete!

THE GOLDEN CROWN
See the list of materials on page 112.

1 Cut the gold paper into two 3 × 7cm (1¼ × 2¾in) pieces and stick them back to back.

2 When the glue is fully dry, trace the outline of the crown on to the back. Mark F and F' with a pin and pierce with a needle.

3 Carefully cut out the crown, just inside the line so you do not see any pencil markings (**a**).

4 Bring the ends together, shaping the crown into a nice circle. Overlap two of the points (see pattern opposite) and stick with a glue gun, then pinch together with a mini clothes peg while the glue dries (**b**).

Attaching the crown

5 Place the crown on the top of the bird's head, with the pierced markings on either side (**c**).

6 Thread a needle with embroidery thread and insert it through mark F', from the outside to the inside (**d**). Ensuring that the crown stays well positioned, insert the needle through the top of the head, from left to right: the entry points will be hidden by the crown (**e**).

7 Insert the needle in the crown at mark F, from the inside to the outside. Pull gently on the ends of the thread to fix the crown on the head (**f**).

8 Using a long needle, pass the end of the thread under the bird's chin, between the stitches catching it to the chest and his neck.

Knot the ends of the elastic together and cut off the excess 2mm (⅟₁₆in) from the knot. Pull the thread round so the knot is hidden under the bird's chin (**g**, **h**).

The golden crown is complete!

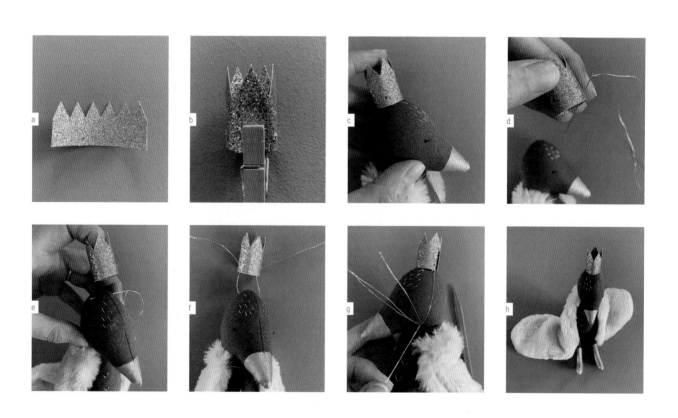

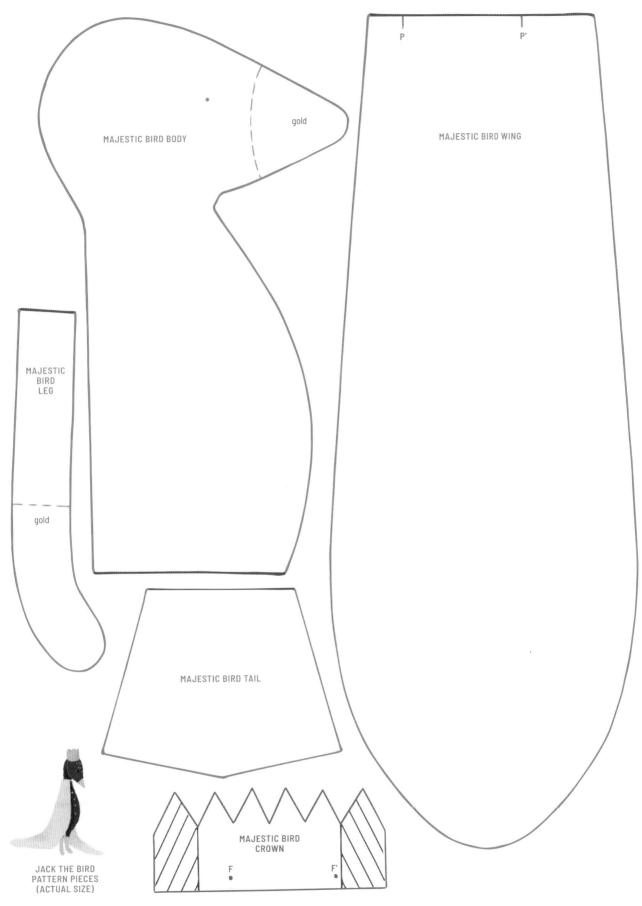

MAJESTIC BIRD BODY

gold

MAJESTIC BIRD WING

P   P'

MAJESTIC
BIRD
LEG

gold

MAJESTIC BIRD TAIL

MAJESTIC BIRD
CROWN

F   F'

JACK THE BIRD
PATTERN PIECES
(ACTUAL SIZE)

119

Robinson and Oscar

MATERIALS

Finished size of Robinson the big lion: 30cm (12in) • Oscar the little lion: 17cm (6¾in)
See page 136 for patterns, other than the pattern for the big lion's body, which is on page 175.
For more details of the techniques used, see the Techniques section on page 10.
The instructions are the same for both models.
The instructions marked in blue or by 🐻 are just for the big lion.
The instructions marked in red or by 🐻 are just for the little lion.

Robinson the big lion and Oscar the little lion
- 🐻 31 × 51cm (12¼ × 20in) linen in light brown
- 🐻 20 × 28cm (7¾ × 11in) cotton in light brown
- 🐻 46 × 6cm (18 × 2½in) shaggy faux fur in light brown
- 🐻 4 × 4cm (1½ × 1½in) shaggy faux fur in light brown
- 🐻 5 × 4cm (2 × 1½in)/🐻 2.5 × 2cm (1 × ¾in) printed cotton in light beige
- 🐻 5 × 4cm (2 × 1½in)/🐻 2.5 × 2cm (1 × ¾in) double-sided fusible interfacing
- 🐻 4 × 3cm (1½ × 1¼in)/🐻 2 × 1cm (¾ × ⅜in) felt in black
- 🐻 8 × 3cm (3¼ × 1¼in)/🐻 6 × 3cm (2⅜ × 1¼in) felt in dark brown
- 🐻 2.5 × 1.5cm (1 × ½in)/🐻 1.5 × 1.5cm (½ × ½in) soluble fabric stabilizer
- Sewing thread in dark brown, black and colours to match the chosen fabric
- 🐻 30cm (11¾in) cotton cordonnet crochet yarn, 0.3mm thick, in light brown
- Long pointed needle
- Toy filling
- 🐻 8 pattern pieces (head parts 1 and 2, arm, muzzle, ear, nose, tail pompom)/🐻 6 pattern pieces (body, head, arm, ear, muzzle, nose, tail)

The big lion's tie
- 11 × 14.5cm (4⁵⁄₁₆ × 5¾in) printed cotton (or poplin, cretonne, polycotton or similar)
- Sewing thread to match the chosen fabric
- Small amount of shirring elastic in gold
- Long pointed needle
- 1 pattern piece (tie)

The big lion's chinos
- 19 × 48cm (7½ × 19in) cotton (or poplin, polycotton, cretonne or similar) in terracotta
- 20cm (7¾in) flat elastic, 5mm (³⁄₁₆in) wide
- Sewing thread to match the chosen fabric
- Safety pin
- 4 pattern pieces (front, back, pocket, pocket lining)

The big lion's trilby hat
- 15 × 9cm (6 × 3½in) boiled wool in dark grey
- Sewing thread in dark grey
- White gel pen
- 1 pattern piece (side)

The little lion's dungarees
- 14 × 28cm (5½ × 11in) printed cotton (or cretonne, poplin, polycotton)
- 8cm (3⅛in) hat elastic
- 2 small buttons, Ø 6mm (¼in), in white
- Sewing thread to match the chosen fabric
- 4 pattern pieces (front, back, bib, shoulder straps)

The little lion's satchel
- 7.5 × 18cm (3 × 7in) leatherette in brown
- 8 × 20cm (3¼ × 7¾in) tissue paper
- Sewing thread in brown
- Cutter
- 4 pattern pieces (satchel, pocket, flap, handle)

The little lion's snood
- 4-ply (fingering) knitting wool, in grey
- Knitting needles 3mm (UK 11, US 2/3)
- Darning needle
- Stitches used: k2 p2 ribbing

Let's use the dead leaves that you
rake up to make a herbarium.
I will teach you the names of the trees
and what I know about their lives.
When you listen to me,
I will grow from you.

BIG LION AND LITTLE LION

See the list of materials on page 120.

🐻 For the big lion:

1 Following the cutting diagram for the big lion, cut the light brown linen into seven pieces:

- 2 pieces 17 × 14.5cm (7 × 5¾in) for the front and back of the head
- 2 pieces 14 × 12cm (5½ × 4¾in) for the arms
- 2 pieces 27 × 11cm (10¾ × 4¼in) for the body
- 1 piece 14 × 2.5cm (5½ × 1in) for the tail.

🐻 For the little lion:

1 Following the cutting diagram for the little lion, cut the cotton into six pieces:

- 2 pieces 10 × 8cm (4 × 3¼in) for the head
- 2 pieces 10 × 8cm (4 × 3¼in) for the arms
- 2 pieces 18 × 6cm (7 × 2½in) for the body.

The face

2 Place the fusible interfacing on the wrong side of the printed cotton and press with an iron to adhere. Still on the wrong side of the printed cotton, trace and cut out the shape of the muzzle. Peel off the protective backing from the fusible interfacing and set to one side for now.

3 Trace and cut out the shape of the nose from the black felt. Set to one side for now.

4 On the wrong side of one of the pieces of 🐻 17 × 14.5cm (7 × 5¾in) linen/🐻 10 × 8cm (4 × 3¼in) cotton, trace the outline of the face (🐻 pattern piece number 1), leaving a space of at least 1cm (⅜in) outside the line.

5 Transfer markings A, B and C and the position of gap O–O'.

CUTTING AND TRACING DIAGRAM BIG LION   CUTTING AND TRACING DIAGRAM LITTLE LION

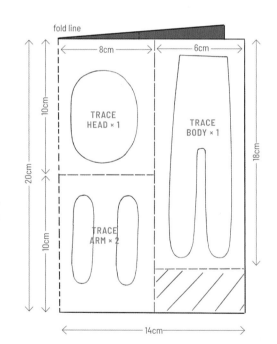

6 Transfer markings A, B and C to the right side of the fabric, using the pin method (see page 33).

7 Cut out the muzzle shape from the pattern piece for the face (🐻 pattern pieces numbers 1 and 2). Place the pattern piece (🐻 number 1) on the right side of the fabric, aligning it with markings A, B and C.

8 Place the fabric muzzle in the hole you have cut out previously, with the fusible side against the 🐻 linen/🐻 cotton. Remove the pattern piece carefully. Press with an iron to hold the muzzle in place.

9 Set your sewing machine to zigzag stitch – stitch length: 0.5mm; stitch width: 🐻 2mm (⅛in)/🐻 1.5mm (½in). Sew around the outline of the muzzle, very close to the edge, starting at the bottom.

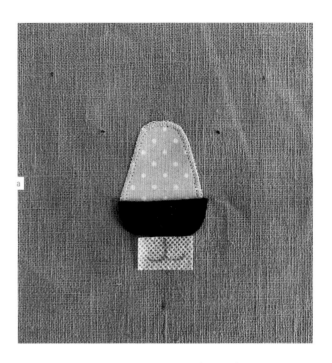

10 Place the felt nose on the bottom of the muzzle, aligning the shapes carefully. Sew around the outside of the nose in straight stitch, 2mm (⅛in) from the edge, without oversewing at the start or finish. Finish with the threads on the wrong side of the work and knot together. Snip off the excess.

11 Place the paper pattern on the right side of the face, according to the markings. Use a pin to mark the position of the eyes on the right side of the fabric (see page 33).

12 Using doubled black thread, embroider a French knot for the eyes (see page 14).

13 Using a single black thread, embroider two small lines above the eyes to make the eyebrows.

14 Place the small piece of soluble fabric stabilizer on the mouth drawn on the pattern piece and trace it.

15 Place the fabric stabilizer on the fabric, just under the felt nose (**a**).

16 With a double thickness of the black thread, embroider the mouth in backstitch over the line traced from the pattern, sewing through both layers of fabric.

17 Place the embroidered part of the face in a little warm water for 1–2 minutes to dissolve the stabilizer. Place the face between two layers of towelling (terrycloth) and press to absorb any excess water. Leave to dry.

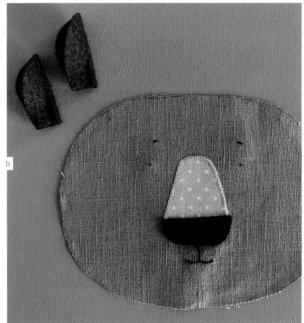

The ears

18 Trace and cut out the shape of the ear twice from the dark brown felt.

19 Fold the ears in half widthways. Starting from the base of the ear, stitch 🐻 1cm (⅜in)/🐻 8mm (⁵⁄₁₆in) up the fold, 🐻 5mm (³⁄₁₆in)/🐻 4mm (³⁄₁₆in) from the edge.

20 Open out the ears: the side with the seam will be at the back of the ear. Set to one side for now (**b**).

The mane

🦁 **For the big lion:**

21 Cut the faux fur into two pieces:
• 1 piece 40 × 6cm (15¾ × 2½in) for the mane
• 1 piece 6 × 6cm (2½ × 2½in) for the tail pompom.
Set this last piece to one side for now.

22 Turn under 1.5cm (½in) at each end of the 40 × 6cm (15¾ × 2½in) band of fur. Sew along the folds, 1cm (⅜in) from the edge.

23 Fold the band in half lengthways, wrong sides together. Tack (baste) the two long sides together 3mm (⅛in) from the edge.

🦁 **For the little lion:**

21 Take the 4 × 4cm (1½ × 1½in) piece and fold it in half, right sides together. Sew along the long open edges, 5mm (³⁄₁₆in) from the edge (**c**).

22 Turn the right way out: you now have a tube.

23 Fold this tube in half widthways. Sew the two ends together, 5mm (³⁄₁₆in) from the edge: this side will be the base of the mane (**d**). Set to one side for now.

Assembling the head, ears and mane

🦁 **For the big lion:**

24 Position pattern number 2 on the right side of the embroidered face, using the cut-out shape of the muzzle to help you. Trace the outline of the pattern piece with a pencil. Transfer marking C to the right side of the fabric and cut around the outline of the head along the line.

25 Now place pattern piece number 1 on the right side of the embroidered face, aligning it with the markings. Place the ears on the pattern piece, the front of the ears against the paper, in accordance with the positions marked. Pin the base of the ears to the fabric of the face to hold them in position (**e**), then remove the pattern piece (**f**).

26 Position and pin the mane against the right side of the face. Align the cut edges of the strip of fur with the outside of the head, edge to edge (**g**). Start by placing one end of the band of fur at mark C and pinning all around the head (**h**).

27 Place the face with the pinned mane on the second 17 × 14.5cm (6¹¹⁄₁₆ × 5¾in) piece of linen, right sides together, leaving a space of at least 1cm (⅜in) all round (**i**). Sew round the head on the line marked, leaving gap O–O' open. You can slightly increase the stitch length to make sewing easier. Sew backwards and forwards a few times at the start and end of the seam to ensure the ends of the gap are secure.

28 Remove the pins and trim the excess fabric from around the head.

29 Carefully turn the head the right way out and stuff firmly. Push the toy filling hard into the whole head so the curves are nicely rounded.

30 Turn under 4mm (³⁄₁₆in) from the edges of gap O–O'.

31 Sew the gap closed, using slip stitch, inserting the needle through each fold in turn and passing it through the mane. Set the head to one side for now.

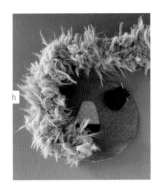
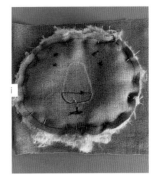

🐻 For the little lion:

24 Position the pattern piece for the head on the embroidered face, using the cut-out shape of the muzzle to help you. Place the ears on the pattern piece, the front of the ears against the paper, in accordance with the positions marked.

25 Pin the base of the ears to the fabric of the face, then remove the pattern piece. Hold in place with a few hand stitches at the base of the ears. Remove the pins.

26 Place the embroidered face on the second piece of 10 × 8cm (4 × 3¼in) cotton, right sides together. Sew round the head on the line marked, leaving gap O–O' open. Go backwards and forwards a few times at the start and end of the seam to ensure the ends of the gap are secure.

27 Cut around the head 3mm (⅛₆in) from the seam and the gap.

28 Carefully turn the head the right way out and stuff firmly. Push the toy filling hard into the whole head so the curves are nicely rounded.

29 Turn under 3mm (⅛₆in) on either side of the gap.

30 Insert and centre the base of the mane in the gap.
Insert around 1cm (⅜in) of the mane inside the head.

31 Sew the gap closed using slip stitch, inserting the needle through each fold in turn and passing it through the mane.
Set the head to one side for now.

The body and the arms

32 On the wrong side of one of the pieces of 🐻 27 × 11cm (10½ × 4¼in) linen/🐻 18 × 6cm (7 × 2½in) cotton, trace the outline of the body once, leaving a space of at least 1cm (⅜in) outside the line.

33 On the wrong side of one of the pieces of 🐻 14 × 12cm (5½ × 4¾in) linen/🐻 10 × 8cm (4 × 3¼in) cotton, trace the outline of the arms twice. Leave a space of at least 1cm (⅜in) around the lines. 🐻 Mark the position of the openings O–O'.

34 Place these pieces of fabric on the second pieces of the same size, right sides together. Sew round the lines on each piece, leaving the openings unstitched (🐻 those at the top of the arms and on the body marked as a red line on the pattern piece) (🐻 gaps O–O' on the arms, and the opening at the top of the body shown by a blue line on the pattern piece).

35 Cut around the pieces 4mm (³⁄₁₆in) 🐻 from the seams and directly against the openings 🐻 from the seams and arm gaps, and directly against the opening on the body.

36 Trim the curves at the base of the legs and arms with pinking shears (j).

37 Turn each piece the right way out and stuff. Push the toy filling well into the legs and body: they must be firm and hold their shape well. Put less toy filling in the arms, so they can bend more easily.

38 Turn under 4mm (³⁄₁₆in) from the edges of each opening. Sew up using slip stitch.

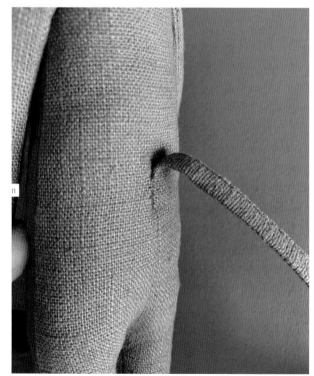

Attaching the head

39 Position the front of the body against the back of the head, using the marking on the pattern to guide you.

40 Sew the head and body together with slip stitch using a single brown thread, sewing in turn through the head and the body (**k, l**). Leave the part under the chin unstitched. Sew backwards and forwards to ensure the seam is secure.

Attaching the arms

🐾 For the big lion:

41 Place one arm along one side of the body so that the top of the arm is 1.5cm (½in) from the top of the body. Centre the top of the arm on the seam line on the side of the body.

42 Sew the arm to the body in slip stitch using a single brown thread, sewing in turn through the body and seam line of the top of the arm (**m**). Sew backwards and forwards to ensure the seam is secure.

43 Do the same for the other arm.

🐾 For the little lion:

41 Attach the arms to the body with cordonnet crochet yarn, following the instructions on page 32.

The little lion is complete!

The tail

🐾 For the big lion:

44 Turn under 8mm (⅜in) from the edges, along the small sides of the 14 × 2.5cm (5½ × 1in) linen band.

45 Fold the band in half lengthways, wrong sides together and mark the fold with an iron. Open the two folded sides and refold each of the edges lengthways to the central fold. Then refold the along the central fold.

46 Sew along the long open edges, 1mm (⅛₆in) from the edge and set to one side for now.

47 Fold the 6 × 6cm (2½ × 2½in) piece of fur in half, right sides together. Pin to hold in place.

48 Place the tail pattern piece on the folded fur: align the top of the tail and the fold with the edges. Trace the outline of the tail in a fine marker pen.

49 Sew along the line, leaving the top of the tail open (red line on the pattern).

50 Cut around the line, 4mm (⅜₆in) from the edge, and turn the right way out: you have a pompom.

51 Turn under 5mm (⅜₆in) on either side of the opening.

52 Insert and centre the band of linen in the opening of the 'pompom' on the side of the cut edge. Insert around 1cm (⅜in) of the tail inside the pompom.

53 Sew along the opening, 3mm (⅛₆in) from the edge.

Attaching the tail

🐾 For the big lion:

54 On the lion's back, place the top of the tail at the mark shown on the pattern: the 'pompom' is pointing towards the head.

55 Sew the tail to the lower back, using slip stitch all around the top of the tail. Point the lion's tail downwards (**n**).

The big lion is complete! (**o**)

o

THE BIG LION'S TIE

See the list of materials on page 120.

1 Following the cutting diagram, cut the fabric into three pieces. You now have:
- 2 pieces 11 × 5.5cm (4¼ × 2¼in) (for the front and back of the tie)
- 1 piece 3.8 × 3.5cm (1½ × 1¼in) (for the knot in the tie).

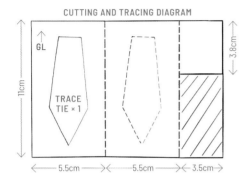

CUTTING AND TRACING DIAGRAM

GL

11cm

3.8cm

TRACE
TIE × 1

← 5.5cm → ← 5.5cm → ← 3.5cm →

2 On the wrong side of one of the pieces of cotton, trace the shape of the tie once. Leave a space of at least 1cm (⅜in) around the line.

3 Place this fabric on the second piece of the same size, right sides together. Sew round the tie on the line marked, leaving the top of the tie open.

4 Cut out the tie, 3mm (⅛in) from the seam and directly against the opening (red line). Turn it the right way out.

5 At the top of the tie, fold the two sides towards the middle (marked X on the pattern). Hold in place with a few stitches sewn by hand over a length of 7mm (¼in), inserting the needle through either side of the tie in turn (**a**).

6 Take the 3.8 × 3.5cm (1½ × 1¼in) piece and fold it in half lengthways, wrong sides together. Mark the fold well with an iron then open out.

7 Fold each of the sides in half, wrong sides together, to the centre fold. Fold one side over the other along the central fold: this will be the knot of the tie.

8 Insert and centre the top of the tie between the two folds of the knot: the two folded parts of the tie should be at the back (**b**).

9 Turn in twice for 5mm (³⁄₁₆in) at the end of the tie knot (**c**, **d**). By hand, using a single thread, sew the whole of the bottom of the knot to the tie using slip stitch. Sew up the top and back of the knot in the same way.

10 Thread the pointed needle with the piece of elastic and push it through the knot of the tie from side to side, pulling the elastic through it (**e**).

11 Adjust the length of the elastic around the lion's neck.

Knot the ends of the elastic together and cut off the excess. The tie is complete! Put the tie on over the lion's feet.

a

b

c

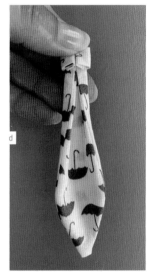

d

e

f

THE BIG LION'S CHINOS

See the list of materials on page 120.

1 Cut out the eight pattern pieces for the chinos, following the instructions in the section Making fabric clothes on page 8.

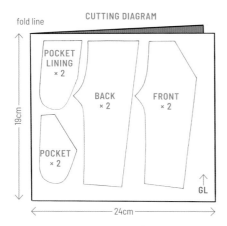

CUTTING DIAGRAM

fold line

POCKET LINING × 2

BACK × 2

FRONT × 2

POCKET × 2

19cm

24cm

GL

2 Overcast all the pieces apart from the two front pieces.

3 Transfer marks P and P' to the wrong side of the front pieces with a small pencil line. Fold each front piece, wrong sides together, along line P–P'.

4 Mark the fold with an iron, then open out the front pieces and overcast.

5 Place a pocket on one of the front pieces, right sides together. Align the edges of the lines marked in red on the patterns.

6 Sew along the red line, 5mm (³⁄₁₆in) from the edge (**a**, **b**).

7 Fold the pocket to the wrong side of the front piece and press with an iron. Topstitch along the seam, 2mm (¹⁄₁₆in) from the edge (**c**, **d**).

8 Place the pocket lining on the pocket, right sides together, aligning the curves. Pin together following this line from mark A to mark B.

9 Sew the curve from A to B, 5mm (³⁄₁₆in) from the edge, ensuring that you do not catch the front of the trousers in the seam (**e**, **f**)!

10 Do the same for the other front piece (**e**, **f**).

11 Place the two front pieces right sides together and sew around the crotch, 5mm (³⁄₁₆in) from the edge. Iron the seams open and set to one side for now.

12 Place the two back pieces right sides together. Put in a pin to mark gap O and O'.

13 Sew around the crotch, 5mm (³⁄₁₆in) from the edge, leaving gap O–O' open. Open out the seam.

14 Place the front and back of the trousers right sides together. Sew along one long side, 5mm (³⁄₁₆in) from the edge (**g**). Open out the seam.

a

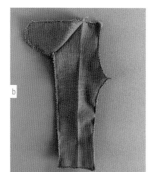

b

c — WRONG SIDE

d — RIGHT SIDE

e

f

g

15 Turn the fabric at the top of the trousers under 1.2cm (½in) from the edge, to create the elasticated waist. Sew around the waist, 1cm (⅜in) from the fold.

16 Thread the elastic into the waist seam, leaving the end sticking out 5mm (³⁄₁₆in) from the entrance to the seam. Secure the start of the elastic, sewing across the point where it enters the waist seam, 3mm (⅛in) from the edge.

17 Pull on the other, unstitched end of the elastic, to reduce the width of the waist to 10cm (4in). Sew across the point where the elastic comes out of the waistband, 3mm (⅛in) from the edge, to secure the elastic in place. Snip off the excess.

18 Sew along the second long side of the trousers, right sides together, 5mm (³⁄₁₆in) from the edge.

19 Turn under 1cm (⅜in) at the bottom of each trouser leg. Sew along the folds, 7mm (¼) from the edge, to make the hems.

20 Sew right round the inside legs, 7mm (¼) from the edge, right sides together. Turn the trousers the right way out.

The chinos are complete! (**h**)

~~~~~~

THE BIG LION'S TRILBY HAT

See the list of materials on page 120.

1 Cut the boiled wool into three pieces:
- 2 pieces 9 × 5cm (3½ × 2in) (for the left and right sides of the hat)
- 1 piece 9 × 5cm (3½ × 2in) (for the brim).

2 On the wrong side of one of the pieces, trace round the pattern piece for the side of the hat.

3 Place this piece of fabric on the second piece of the same size, right sides together. Sew around the outline of the hat on the line marked, leaving the straight base of the hat open.

4 Cut out the hat, 3mm (⅛in) from the seam and directly against the gap.

5 Turn the hat the right way out and shape it by pulling the two sides apart.

6 Position the hat on the third piece of boiled wool, the edges of the opening centred on the rectangle of fabric. Pin around the base of the hat to hold it in place (**a**).

7 By hand, sew the two parts together with backstitch all round the pinned circumference, 2mm (¹⁄₁₆in) from the edge, forming a small brim all round (**b**).

8 Cut the excess fabric from the rectangle to shape the brim, around 8mm (⁵⁄₁₆in) from the sides of the hat (**c**, **d**).

The trilby hat is complete! Put it on top of the lion's head.

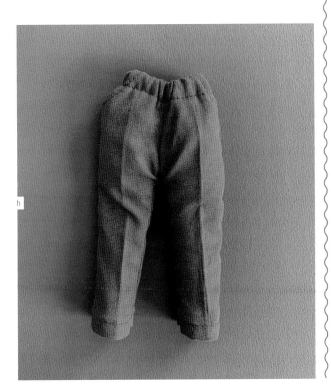

THE LITTLE LION'S DUNGAREES

See the list of materials on page 120.

1 Cut out the eight pattern pieces for the dungarees, following the instructions in the section Making fabric clothes on page 8. Overcast the two front pieces and the two back pieces.

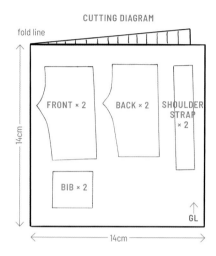

CUTTING DIAGRAM

fold line

FRONT × 2

BACK × 2

SHOULDER STRAP × 2

BIB × 2

14cm

14cm

GL

The shoulder straps

2 Turn under 5mm (³⁄₁₆in) at one end of each of the rectangles for the shoulder straps. Fold them in half lengthways, wrong sides together. Mark the fold in the middle with an iron, then open out (**a**).

3 Fold each side in half, wrong sides together, to the central fold, then fold one side over the other at the central fold (**b**).

4 Sew along the open edge, 1mm (¹⁄₁₆in) from the edge.

The bib

5 Place the pieces of the bib right sides together and use a pencil to transfer the markings indicating the position of the shoulder straps.

6 Insert the shoulder straps between the two layers of fabric where marked. The ends of the shoulder straps should stick out 5mm (³⁄₁₆in) from the top of the bib.

7 Sew around the bib, 3mm (⅛in) from the edge, leaving the bottom of the bib open (blue line) (**c**).

8 Turn the bib the right way out and overcast the bottom, sewing through both layers of fabric.

9 Mark the centre of the bottom of the bib with a pin and set to one side for now.

The front of the dungarees

10 Transfer markings A and A' to the front pieces of the dungarees. Overlap these marks on each piece, right sides together, to create the tucks.

11 Sew a few stitches along the top of the front pieces, 3mm (⅛in) from the edge to hold the tucks in place.

12 Place the front pieces right sides together and sew around the crotch 5mm (³⁄₁₆in) from the edge. Press the seams open with an iron.

13 Place the bib on the front of the trousers, right sides together, aligning the bottom of the bib with the top of the trousers, edge to edge, and the centre of the bib with the centre front of the trousers.

14 Sew along the bib, 8mm (⁵⁄₁₆in) from the edge (**d**). Set to one side for now, with the bib still folded down against the front of the trousers.

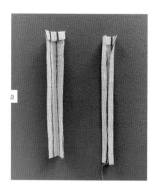

a

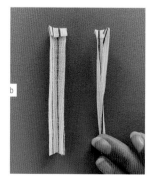

b

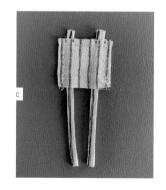

c

d

The back of the dungarees

15 Place the back pieces right sides together and sew around the crotch, 5mm (³⁄₁₆in) from the edge. Press the seams open with an iron.

16 Turn under 8mm (⁵⁄₁₆in) along the top of the back. Sew along 5mm (³⁄₁₆in) from the edge to make the hem for the elasticated waist.

17 Insert the piece of elastic into the waistband, allowing its end to stick out 5mm (³⁄₁₆in) from the entrance to the seam. Secure the start of the elastic, sewing across the point where it enters the waist seam, 3mm (⅛in) from the edge (**e**).

18 Pull on the other, unstitched end of the elastic, to reduce the width of the waist to 3.5cm (1⅜in). Sew across the point where the elastic comes out of the waistband, 3mm (⅛in) from the edge, to secure the elastic in place. Snip off the excess.

Assembling the front and back

19 Place the front and back of the dungarees right sides together: the seam between the bib and the front of the trousers should extend 8mm (⁵⁄₁₆in) beyond the top of the back.

20 Sew along the long sides of the trousers, 5mm (³⁄₁₆in) from the edge: from the bottom of the legs to the top of the elasticated waist. Press the seams open with an iron.

21 Turn under 8mm (⁵⁄₁₆in) along the bottom of each leg and sew along the folds, 5mm (³⁄₁₆in) from the edge to make the hems.

22 Sew around the inside legs, 5mm (³⁄₁₆in) from the edge.

23 Turn the dungarees the right way out, leaving the bib downwards against the front of the trousers. The sides of the front top of the dungarees pull inwards, wrong sides together. Sew into place with a little stitch in the seam.

24 Bring the bib up: the bottom of the bib swings down and is positioned against the seam allowance of the elasticated waist. Hand sew each side of the bottom of the bib to the waistband of the trousers (see pictures **f** to **h** of Olivia's dungarees, page 82).

Finishing touches

25 Slip the dungarees on the lion. Cross the shoulder straps at the back and sew them on to the wrong side of the elasticated waistband, 1cm (⅜in) from their ends.

26 Sew on two small buttons to hide the stitches (**f**).

The dungarees are complete!

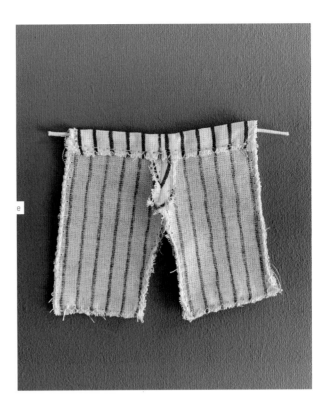

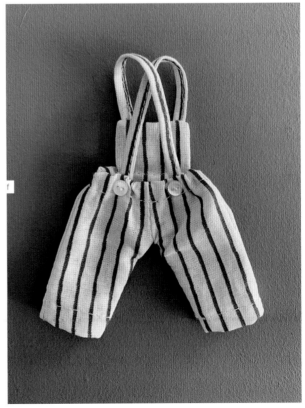

THE LITTLE LION'S SATCHEL

See the list of materials on page 120.

1 Trace the four satchel pattern pieces and cut them out of the leatherette.

2 Use the point of a pencil to transfer markings A–A' and B–B' to the wrong side of the leatherette pocket. Using the cutter, make two slits by cutting the leatherette between A and A' and between B and B'.

3 Identify the position of C–C' and D–D' on the right side of the satchel and mark them simply with a pin.

4 Place the pocket on the satchel, wrong side to right side, such that the top of the pocket is parallel to side E'–F' of the satchel and 1cm (⅜in) from the edge. The sides of the pocket should be centred 1cm (⅜in) from the edges of sides E–E' and F–F' of the satchel.

5 The presser foot does not slide over the right side of leatherette very effectively: tissue paper can solve the problem. Place the tissue paper on top of the satchel and the pocket and sew round the outside of the pocket in straight stitch, 2mm (¹⁄₁₆in) from the edge, leaving the top of the pocket open.

In the following steps, you simply need to lift up the tissue paper and place the pieces of fabric underneath it.

6 Position the handle on the satchel, wrong side to right side, aligning the small sides of the handle with marks C–C' and D–D'. Sew along the small sides of the handle, 2mm (¹⁄₁₆in) from the edge.

7 Place the small square side of the tab on the satchel, wrong side to right side, at the position shown on the pattern. Sew along the small side of the tab in straight stitch 5mm (³⁄₁₆in) from the edge.

8 Remove the tissue paper gently, tearing it along the seams (**a**).

9 Fold the satchel, right sides together, and align mark E with E' and mark F with F'. Sew along these two sides of the satchel, 3mm (⅛in) from the edge.

10 Clip the corners at the bottom of the satchel and turn it the right way out.

To close, insert the tab through the two slits in the pocket (**b**). The satchel is complete!

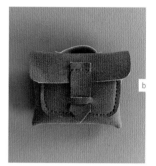

THE LITTLE LION'S SNOOD

See the list of materials on page 120.

1 Cast on 38 sts.
- Rows 1–27: k2 p2.
- Row 28: k all sts, casting off loosely.

2 Use the working yarn to sew the two shorter edges of the snood together to form a tube (**a**, **b**).

3 Work in the ends of the yarn.

The snood is complete! Slip it round the little lion's neck and fold over the top of the snood.

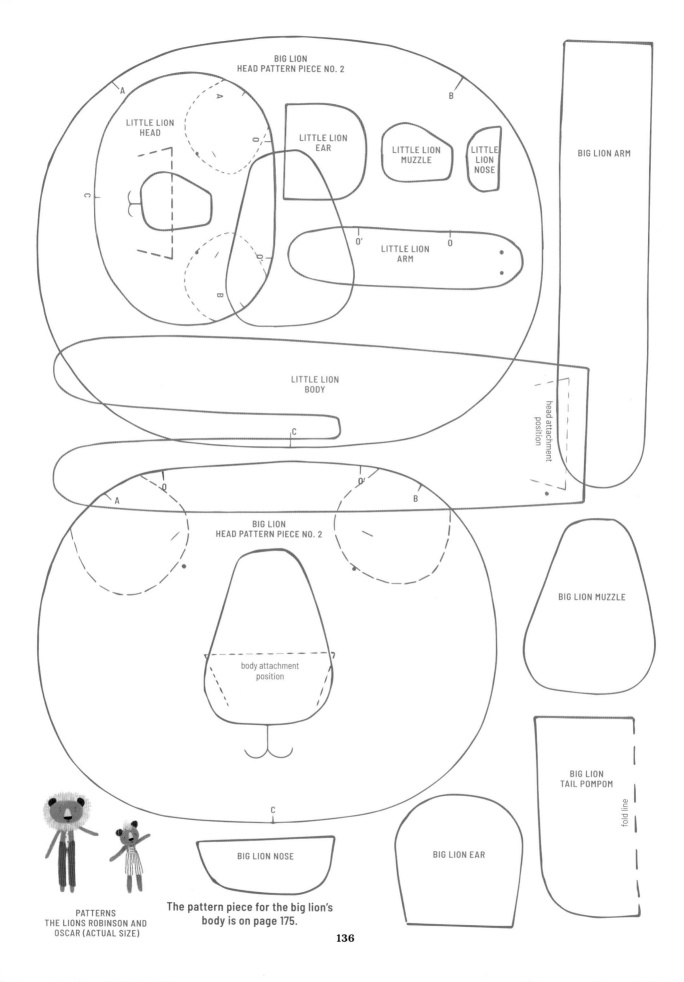

BIG LION
HEAD PATTERN PIECE NO. 2

LITTLE LION
HEAD

LITTLE LION
EAR

LITTLE LION
MUZZLE

LITTLE
LION
NOSE

BIG LION ARM

LITTLE LION
ARM

LITTLE LION
BODY

head attachment
position

BIG LION
HEAD PATTERN PIECE NO. 2

body attachment
position

BIG LION MUZZLE

BIG LION
TAIL POMPOM

fold line

BIG LION NOSE

BIG LION EAR

PATTERNS
THE LIONS ROBINSON AND
OSCAR (ACTUAL SIZE)

The pattern piece for the big lion's
body is on page 175.

136

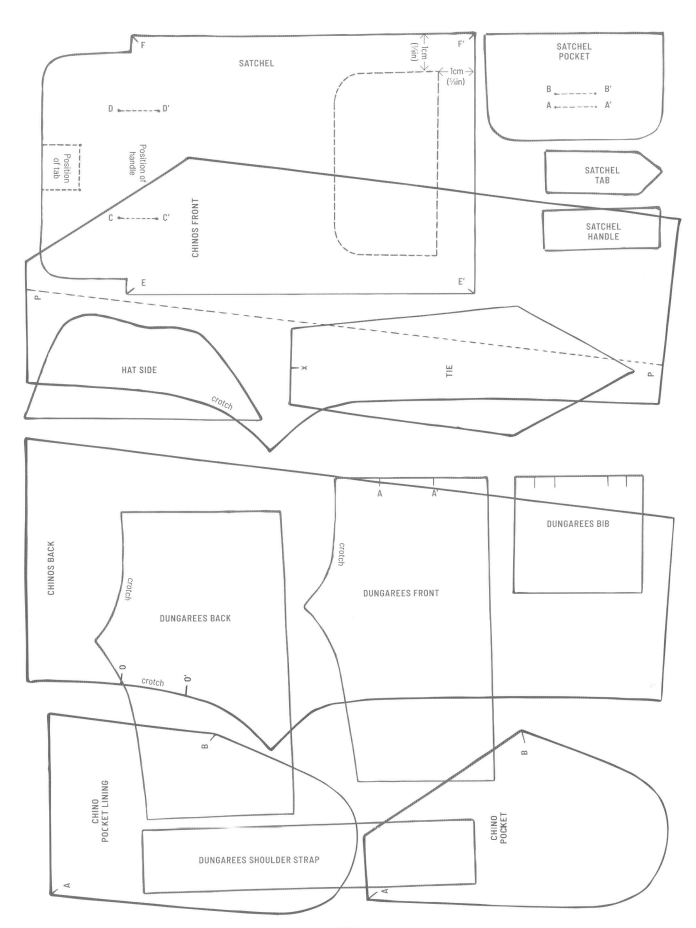

Mina the little cat

MATERIALS

Finished size of the little cat: 22cm (8½in) • chest: 24cm (9½in)
See pages 144 and 145 for patterns and illustrations, other than the pattern for the chest which is on page 44.
For more details of the techniques used, see the Techniques section on page 10.
The instructions for sewing Mina's dress together are the same as those for Emilie the girl hare.
The instructions marked 🐱 are just for Mina's dress. Those marked 🐰 are just for Emilie's dress.

Mina the little cat
× See the list of materials on page 48

Mina's 🐱 and Emilie's 🐰 dress
× 🐱 12 × 45cm (4¾ × 17¾in) printed cotton
(or poplin, cambric, cretonne, polycotton) /
🐰 11 × 64cm (4¼ × 25¼in) double cotton gauze
× 🐱 44cm (17½in)/🐰 50cm (20in) ribbon, 7mm (¼in)
wide, in a colour to match your chosen fabric
× Sewing thread to match the chosen fabric and ribbon

The cape
× 18 × 15cm (7 × 6in) velvet in dark green
× 24 × 20cm (9½ × 7¾in) cotton fabric in ecru
× 2 pieces of 10cm (4in) ribbon, 7mm (¼in) wide, in bronze
× White pencil or gel pen

The knickers
× 4-ply (fingering) woollen yarn, in off-white
and mustard yellow
× Crochet hook 3mm (UK 11, US 2/3)
× Darning needle
× Marker ring
× Stitches used: chain stitch (ch) • double
crochet (dc) • slip stitch (sl st)

The crown headband
× 3 × 7cm (1¼ × 2¾in) thick fabric in gold
× Shirring elastic in gold
× Sewing thread to match fabric
× Long pointed needle
× 1 pattern (crown)

The flower headband
× Pearl cotton thread in bronze yellow, no. 8
× Shirring elastic in gold
× Crochet hook 1.75mm (UK 15/US 00)
× Long pointed needle
× Stitches used: chain stitch (ch) • double
crochet (dc) • half-treble (htr) • treble (tr)

The shawl
× See the list of materials on page 50

The windmill
× 15 × 15cm (6 × 6in) sparkly gold paper
× Mini split pin in black
× Small 11cm (4¼in) wooden stick (skewer or twig)
× Glue gun
× Pencil
× Scissors
× Thick needle
× Scrap of sandpaper
× 1 pattern (sail)

The chest
× See the list of materials on page 36

My little cat
to dress up

Play and dream!

To make the world more beautiful,
I dress up and write theatre plays.
I have made my little artist's dressing
room from a simple cardboard box.
This is where I go to change my
costume and invent my universe.

MINA THE LITTLE CAT

See the list of materials on page 48.
The instructions for making Mina are the same
as for The Rainbow Club Friends cats on page 52.

THE DRESS

See the list of materials on page 138.
The instructions marked 🎃 are
just for Mina's dress. Those marked
🐱 are just for Emilie's dress.

1 Overcast all edges of the fabric rectangle.

2 In straight stitch, sew a line of gathers along one of the long sides, 1cm (⅜in) from the edge: this will be the top of the dress. Sew a second line of gathers parallel to the first, 1.5cm (½in) from the edge (for more detail, see Making a row of gathers, page 13).

3 Pull gently on the gathering threads and reduce the width of the top of the dress to 🎃 8cm (3¼in) 🐱 10cm (4in) (**a**, **b**). Knot the gathering threads in pairs and cut off the excess threads.

4 Position the ribbon on the rows of gathers. Extend 🎃 18cm (7in)/ 🐱 20cm (7¾in) of the ribbon either side of the dress.

5 Sew around the ribbon 1mm (¹⁄₁₆in) from the top (**c**) and 1mm (¹⁄₁₆in) from the bottom.

The dress is complete! Tie it round the character's neck.

~~~

THE CAPE

See the list of materials on page 138.

1 On the wrong side of the velvet rectangle, on the long side, draw a first mark 6cm (2½in) from the edge and a second mark 6cm (2½in) beyond the first. These two markings indicate the position of the gap.

2 Draw a mark on each short side, opposite each other, 3cm (1¼in) from the edge (on the same side as the gap). These two marks show where the ribbons will be positioned.

3 Place this fabric on the rectangle of cotton, right sides together. Centre the velvet rectangle on the cotton rectangle: the fabric allowances around the velvet rectangle should be large enough to allow for it shifting while it is being hemmed.

4 Insert the ribbons between the two layers of fabric in accordance with the marks, ensuring that they extend around 1cm (⅜in) beyond the edges of the fabrics (**a**). Pin to hold in place.

5 Sew all round the velvet rectangle, 5mm (³⁄₁₆in) from the edge, leaving the gap open (**b**).

6 Trim the piece of cotton around the velvet rectangle and clip the corners (**b**).

7 Turn the cape the right way out, pushing the corners out carefully.

8 Turn under 5mm (³⁄₁₆in) on either side of the gap, and sew up using slip stitch.

The cape is complete! Knot it around the character's neck, with the collar folded to the outside.

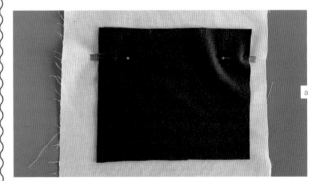

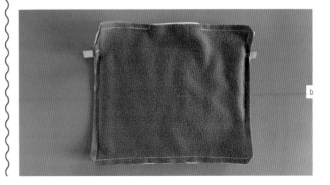

141

THE KNICKERS

See the list of materials on page 138 and the basic crocheting instructions on page 16.

1 The knickers are worked from the waist down.

Round 1: ch 26 in off-white, join into a ring with sl st (= 26 sts). Continue working in rounds.

Round 2: 1 dc in each st (= 26 sts).

Round 3: 1 dc in each st (= 26 sts) in yellow.

Rounds 4–7: 1 dc in each st (= 26 sts) in off-white.

Round 8: 1 dc in the first 25 sts. Insert the hook through st 26 then st 13. Work 1 sl st in the 2 sts together to form the crotch (**a**, **b**).

2 Fasten off and snip the tails.

3 In the yellow yarn, work 1 dc in each of the 26 st around the waist (adjustable ring) (= 26 sts) (**c**).

4 Fasten off with 1 sl st and work in the ends of the yarn.

5 In the yellow yarn, work 1 dc in each of the 13 sts around each thigh (= 13 sts and 13 sts).

6 Fasten off with 1 sl st and work in the ends of the yarn.

The knickers are complete! (**d**)

THE CROWN HEADBAND

See the list of materials on page 138.

1 Cut the gold fabric into two 3 × 3.5cm (1¼ × 1½in) pieces.

2 On the wrong side of one of the pieces, trace the outline of the crown and cut out along the line.

3 Place this side of the crown on the second piece of gold fabric, wrong sides together. Sew around the outside, 1mm (¹⁄₁₆in) from the edge, without oversewing at the start or finish (**a**).

4 Bring the threads out on the back of the crown (**b**). Knot them together and cut off the excess, 1mm (¹⁄₁₆in) from the knot.

5 Trim the fabric around the crown.

6 Using a long pointed needle, insert the elastic between two seam stitches on one side of the crown, bringing it out in the seam on the other side (see the markings on the pattern) (**c**).

7 Adjust the headband around the cat's head.

Knot the ends of the elastic together and cut off the excess.

The crown headband is complete!

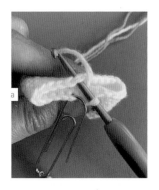
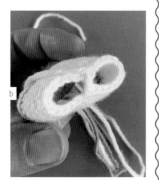
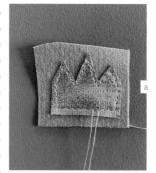

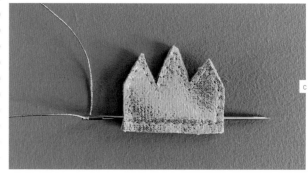

THE FLOWER HEADBAND

See the list of materials on page 138.

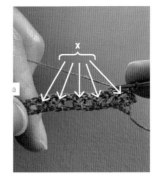

1 The headband is worked in rows.

Row 1: ch 25 and place marker ring in last st.

Work 4 ch and 1 tr in the st of the chain marked by the ring. *Skip 2 sts and work 1 tr in the next st, 1 ch then 1 tr still in the same st*.

Rep from * to * to end of chain. You now have the crochet work shown in picture **a**.

Row 2: flip the work over and work 1 ch. In each triangular hole along the top (marked with an arrow on picture a), work *1 dc, 1 htr, 3 tr, 1 htr, 1 dc*: this sequence forms a petal.

Rep from * to * to end of row (**b, c**)

2 Fasten off with 1 sl st and work in the ends of the yarn (**b, c**).

Finishing touches

3 Roll up the petals to form the flower (**d**). Using the working yarn, sew all the layers of the petals together, through the base of the flower (**e**). Knot the ends of the yarn together and cut off the excess.

4 Thread the gold elastic through the base of the flower using a long, pointed needle (**f**). Adjust it around the cat's head. Knot the ends of the elastic together and cut off the excess.

~~~~~

THE SHAWL

See the list of materials on page 50.
The instructions for making the shawl are the same as for Jeanne's shawl on page 69.

THE WINDMILL

See the list of materials on page 138.

1 On the wrong side of the gold paper, trace round the pattern pieces for the sails of the windmill five times. Cut out the sails, just inside the line so you do not see any pencil markings.

2 Use a pin to transfer marks A and B to each sail. Pierce the marks carefully using a thick needle, ensuring you do not tear the paper.

3 Insert the split pin through mark A on all the sails, pushing it through to the back of the paper: the sails overlap, one on top of the other, in the same direction (**a**, **b**, **c**).

4 Arrange the sails as shown below (**d**).

5 Take hold of the first sail inserted and fold it back on itself. Insert the split pin through mark B, pushing it through to the back of the paper (**e**, **f**).

6 Do the same for all the other sails, following the same order. Open out the legs of the split pin to hold the sails in place.

7 Take the wooden stick and, if necessary, sand the ends to get rid of any sharp edges.

8 Place a dot of hot glue on the open ends of the split pin and glue one end of the stick on top of it (**g**).

The windmill is finished! (**h**)

THE CHEST

See the list of materials on page 36.
To make the chest, use the patterns and instructions for Mini-rabbit's bed on pages 44-45.
Once you have finished making the chest and glued on the illustration, knot the ribbon around it.

You can download these illustrations at actual size from
www.bookmarkedhub.com

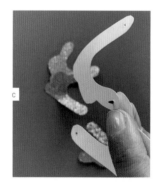
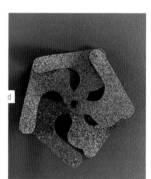

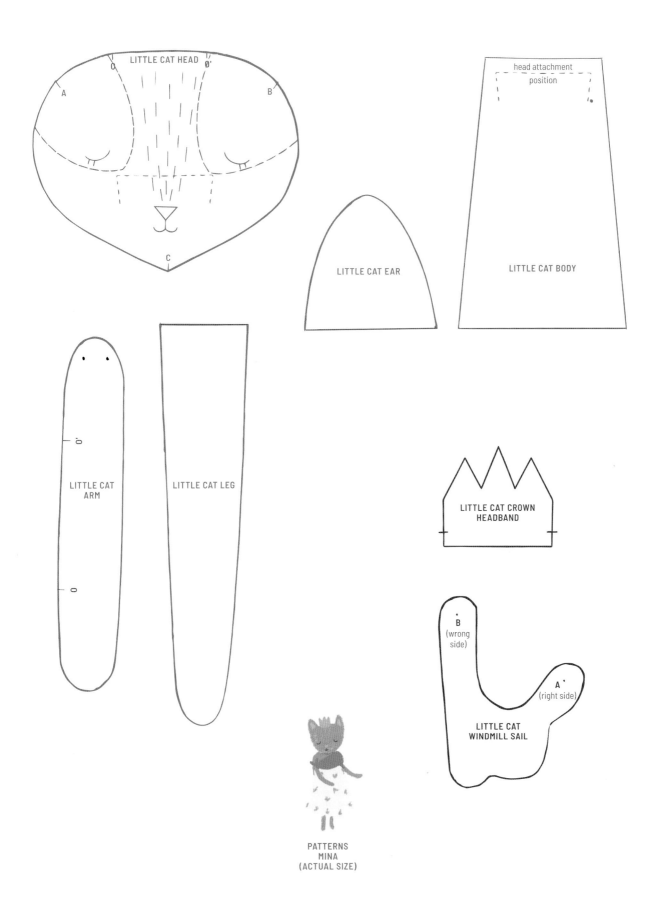

LITTLE CAT HEAD

A

B

C

0

0'

head attachment position

LITTLE CAT EAR

LITTLE CAT BODY

LITTLE CAT ARM

0'

0

LITTLE CAT LEG

LITTLE CAT CROWN HEADBAND

B
(wrong side)

A
(right side)

LITTLE CAT WINDMILL SAIL

PATTERNS
MINA
(ACTUAL SIZE)

145

Tom and Emilie

MATERIALS

Finished size: 22cm (8½in)
See page 159 for patterns, other than the
pattern for the pointy hat which is on page 89.
For more details of the techniques used, see the Techniques section on page 10.

The hares
× 32 × 40cm (12½ × 15¾in) linen in sand or hazel,
depending on which hare you are making
× 2 pieces of 18 × 9cm (7 × 3½in) cotton voile in ecru
× Sewing thread in black and sable or hazel
× Cotton cordonnet crochet yarn, 0.3mm thick, in ecru
× Toy filling
× Blusher in pink and apricot
× Long pointed needle
× 4 pattern pieces (body, leg, arm, ear)

The pointy hat
× See the list of materials on page 50

Tom's shorts
× 2 colours of 4-ply (fingering) yarn,
in white and denim blue
× 2 tiny buttons, Ø 5mm (³⁄₁₆in), in white
× Crochet hook 3mm (UK 11, US 2/3)
× Marker ring
× Darning needle
× Stitches used: chain stitch (ch) • double
crochet (dc) • slip stitch (sl st)

Tom's bow tie
× 10 × 5.5cm (4 × 2¼in) cotton (or poplin, cretonne,
polycotton or similar) in mustard yellow
× Sewing thread in mustard yellow
× A small amount of toy filling
× 12cm (4¾in) round elastic, Ø 2mm (¹⁄₁₆in), in gold

Emilie's ruff
× 11 × 64cm (4¼ × 25¼in) lace in ecru
× Sewing thread in ecru
× 15cm (6in) round elastic, Ø 2mm (¹⁄₁₆in), in white
× Safety pin

Emilie's dress
× See the list of materials on page 138

Emilie's knickers
× 5-ply (sport) crochet wool, in pale pink
× Crochet hook 3mm (UK 11, US 2/3)
× Marker ring
× Darning needle
× Stitches used: chain stitch (ch) • double
crochet (dc) • slip stitch (sl st)

No-one on earth knows me like you do.
My childhood, full of our games and shared laughter, will
help me to grow even when I am no longer so small.

THE BOY AND GIRL HARES

See the list of materials on page 146.

The brother and sister hares are made in exactly the same way as each other. Only their colour and outfits differ.

1 Following the cutting diagram, cut the linen into eight pieces:
- 2 pieces 14 × 11cm (5½ × 4¼in) for the left and right sides of the body
- 2 pieces 18 × 9cm (7 × 3½in) for the ears
- 2 pieces 14 × 9cm (5½ × 3½in) for the arms
- 2 pieces 18 × 11cm (7 × 4¼in) for the legs.

The ears

2 Trace the outline of the ear on the wrong side of the rectangle of the two pieces of cotton voile, leaving an allowance of at least 1cm (⅜in) outside the traced lines, except at the base of the ears.

3 Place these pieces of fabric on the two pieces of linen of the same size, right sides together. Sew around each ear on the line marked, leaving the base of the ear open.

4 Cut around the ears, 3mm (⅛in) from the seams and directly against the openings (red line). Turn the ears the right way out.

5 Turn under 5mm (³⁄₁₆in) on either side of the openings in the ears.

6 At the base of the ears, fold the sides to the middle, inside to inside (cotton voile against cotton voile) (**a**).

7 Sew up the openings in slip stitch, sewing alternately through the two layers at the base of the ear. At the end of the seam, finish with a knot then insert the needle again next to the knot and bring it out on the other side, where you started sewing (**b**, **c**). Do not cut the thread, you will use it later to sew the ears to the head.

CUTTING AND TRACING DIAGRAM

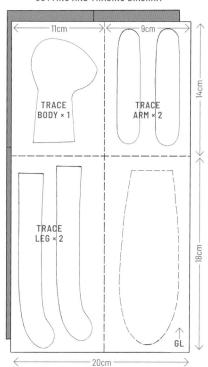

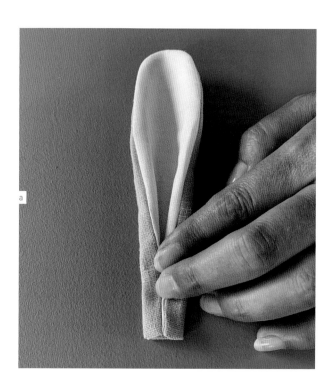

The arms

8 On the wrong side of one of the pieces of 14 × 9cm (5½ × 3½in) linen, trace the outline of the arms twice, leaving a space of at least 1cm (⅜in) outside the lines. Transfer the position of gaps O–O' to each of the arms.

9 Place this piece of fabric on the second piece of the same size, right sides together. Sew round each arm on the lines marked, leaving the gaps open.

10 Cut around the arms, 3mm (⅛in) from the seams and the gaps. Turn the arms the right way out.

11 Stuff them lightly: the arms must not be stiff.

12 Turn under 3mm (⅛in) on either side of gaps and sew up using slip stitch. Set to one side for now.

The legs

13 On the wrong side of one of the pieces of 18 × 11cm (7 × 4¼in) linen, trace the outline of the leg twice, leaving a space of at least 1cm (⅜in) outside the line, except at the base of the legs.

14 Place this piece of fabric on the second piece of the same size. Sew round each leg on the lines marked, leaving the base of the legs open.

15 Cut around the legs, 3mm (⅛in) from the seams and directly against the openings (red line). Turn them the right way out.

16 Stuff them very firmly and set to one side for now.

The body and the head

17 On the wrong side of one of the pieces of 14 × 11cm (5½ × 4¼in) linen, trace the outline of the body, leaving a space of at least 1cm (⅜in) outside the line, except at the base of the body.

18 Use a pin to transfer the position of the eye and marks R and R' marking the position of the ear to the right side of the fabric (see technique on page 33).

19 Place this piece of fabric on the second piece of the same size. Sew round the traced outline of the body, leaving the bottom edge open.

20 Cut around the body, 3mm (⅛in) from the seams and directly against the opening (red line). Turn your hare the right way out.

21 Use a pin to transfer the position of the eye and marks R and R' through the fabric so they are marked on the other side of the face.

22 Stuff the body firmly. Push the toy filling hard up against the seams so the curves are nicely rounded.

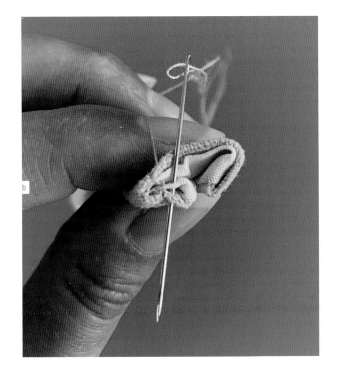

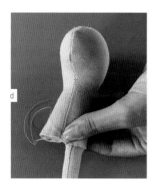  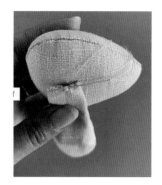 

Attaching the legs

23 Turn under 5mm (³⁄₁₆in) from the two edges of the opening in the body. Pinch the edge of the gap together so the two hem lines are against each other.

24 Insert the top of one leg in the opening: position the seam in the middle of the leg to the front of the hare and the leg against the side of the body (**d**).

25 Start to sew the opening in the body closed, using slip stitch, inserting the needle alternately through each fold followed by the leg.

26 Once the first leg is attached, insert the second in the opening and finish the seam.

Attaching the ears

27 Place one ear against the head, aligning the ends of the base of the ear with marks R and R'. Sew on the ear with slip stitch, sewing alternately through the head and the external fold of the base of the ear (**e, f, g**).

28 Finish with a knot and work the thread into the head.

29 Sew on the second ear on the opposite side.

Attaching the arms

30 Position the arms on either side of the body in accordance with the markings. Using a needle threaded with doubled cordonnet crochet yarn, attach the arms on either side of the body, following the instructions on page 32.

Finishing touches

31 Use doubled black thread, knotted at the ends, to embroider the eyes. To do this, insert the needle into the head seam, between two stitches. Bring out the needle at the location of the eye and pull gently on the thread to pull the knot into the head. Embroider the eye with a French knot (see page 14), then insert the needle at the base of the stitch. Bring the needle back out at the location of the second eye and embroider it with another French knot. Insert the needle in the base of the stitch to work in the thread. Snip off the excess.

32 Using a single black thread, embroider a little V-shape in backstitch for the nose. Finish with a little knot in the centre of the V. Take the thread into the head and pull gently on it to hide the knot in the central seam of the face.

33 Add a little apricot blusher to the nose and pink blusher to the cheeks.

The hare is complete!

THE POINTY HAT

See the list of materials on page 50.
The instructions for making the pointy hat are the same as those for Jeanne's hat on page 73.

~~~~~~~

TOM'S BOW TIE

See the list of materials on page 146.

1 Cut the cotton rectangle into two rectangles measuring 7.5 × 5.5cm (3 × 2¼in) and 2.5 × 5.5cm (1 × 2¼in).

2 On the big rectangle, mark a 3cm (1¼in) gap in the middle of one of the small sides.

3 Fold the rectangle in half widthways, right sides together.

4 Sew all round the rectangle, 3mm (⅛in) from the edge, leaving the gap open. Clip the corners (**a**).

5 Turn the right way out and stuff.

6 Turn under 3mm (⅛in) on either side of the gap and sew up using slip stitch.

7 Fold the small rectangle in half lengthways, wrong sides together. Mark the fold in the middle with an iron, then open out.

8 Fold each of the sides in half, wrong sides together, to the centre fold. Fold one side over the other along the central fold (**a**).

9 Pinch the two long sides of the stuffed rectangle together (**b**).

10 Wrap the narrow band around the big stuffed rectangle, pulling it tight to emphasize the pinch (**c**).

11 On the back of the bow tie, turn in the end of the narrow band of fabric by 5mm (³⁄₁₆in).

12 Place this end on the other end and stitch together by hand (**d**).

13 Insert the elastic under the narrow band of fabric, on the back of the bow tie (**e**).

14 Adjust the length of the elastic around the hare's neck. Knot the ends of the elastic together. Snip off the excess (**f**).

The bow tie is complete! Pull it on over the hare's legs and slip it up over his shoulders.

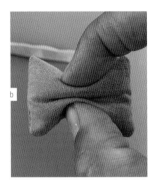
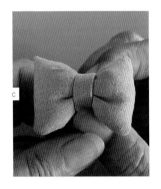
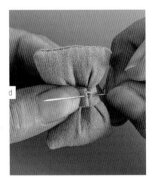
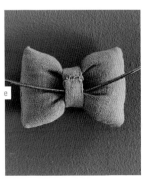
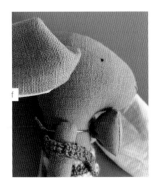

TOM'S SHORTS

See the list of materials on page 146 and the basic crocheting instructions on pages 16–24.

The shorts

1 The shorts are worked in the round from the waist.

Round 1: ch 26 in white, join into a ring with sl st.

Round 2: 1 dc in each st (= 26 sts) in white.

Rounds 3 and 4: 1 dc in each st in blue (= 26 sts).

Rounds 5–10: alternating 2 rounds in white and 2 rounds in blue, 1 dc in each st (= 26 sts).

Round 11: in blue, 1 dc in the first 25 sts. Insert the hook through st 26 then st 14 of the round. 1 sl st in these two sts together to form the crotch (**a, b**).

The shorts are divided in two.

2 Continue by crocheting one of the two legs first.

Round 12: in blue, 1 dc in each st (= 13 sts) (**c**).

Rounds 13–16: alternating 2 rounds in white and 2 rounds in blue, 1 dc in each st (= 13 sts).

3 Fasten off with 1 sl st and work in the ends of the yarn.

4 Return to the second leg at round 12 and crochet in the same way (**d**).

The braces

5 These start from the back of the shorts and are worked in rows, with just the blue yarn.

6 With the back of the shorts facing you, mark the middle of the back with a marker on the last round (**e**).

First brace

7 From the third st, work 3 dc in blue (= 3 sts) (**f, g, h**).

Row 2: *Flip work over, 1 ch 2 dc* (= 2 sts).

Rows 3–22: rep from * to * (= 2 sts).

8 Fasten off with 1 sl st and work in the ends of the yarn.

Second brace

9 Row 1: count 4 sts to the right from the marker ring (**i**). From the fifth st, work 3 dc (=3 sts) (**j**).

Row 2: *Flip work over, 1 ch 2 dc* (= 2 sts).

Rows 3–22: rep from * to * (= 2 sts).

10 Fasten off with 1 sl st and work in the ends of the yarn.

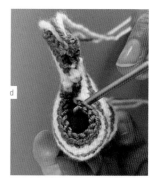

Finishing touches

11 Cross the braces (**k**). Sew the ends to the front of the shorts, 2cm (⅜in) from where each brace starts at the back (**l**).

12 Sew a small button to each brace, 5mm (³⁄₁₆in) from their ends (**m**). The shorts with braces are complete!

EMILIE'S KNICKERS

See the list of materials on page 146 and the basic crocheting instructions on pages 16–24.

1 The knickers are worked in the round from the waist.
Round 1: ch 25, join into a ring with sl st. (= 25 sts) (**a**).
Rounds 2–6: 1 dc in each st (= 25 sts).
2 Round 7: 1 dc in first 24 st. Insert hook through st 25 then st 12 of the round. 1 sl st in these two sts together to form the crotch (**b**, **c**, **d**).
3 Cut the yarn and work in the ends.
The knickers are complete!

EMILIE'S RUFF

See the list of materials on page 146.

1 Fold the lace rectangle in half widthways, wrong sides together. Align the two short edges.

2 Sew the short edges together, 5mm (3⁄16in) from the edge. Trim the seam allowance to 2mm (1⁄16in).

3 Turn the tube right sides together (**a**) and sew along the seam made previously, 5mm (3⁄16in) from the edge.

4 Fold the tube in half along its whole length, wrong sides together, aligning the edges.

5 Sew along the fold, 1cm (3⁄8in) from the edge, leaving a 2cm (3⁄4in) gap through which you can insert the elastic (**b**).

6 Thread the elastic into the hem using a safety pin (**c**).

7 Adjust the circumference of the ruff around the hare's neck. Knot the ends of the elastic and cut off the excess (**d**, **e**).

8 Sew up the gap by continuing the hemline.

The ruff is complete!

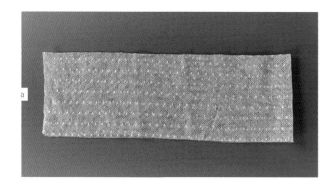

EMILIE'S DRESS

See the list of materials on page 138.
The instructions for making up the shawl are the same as for Mina's dress on page 141.

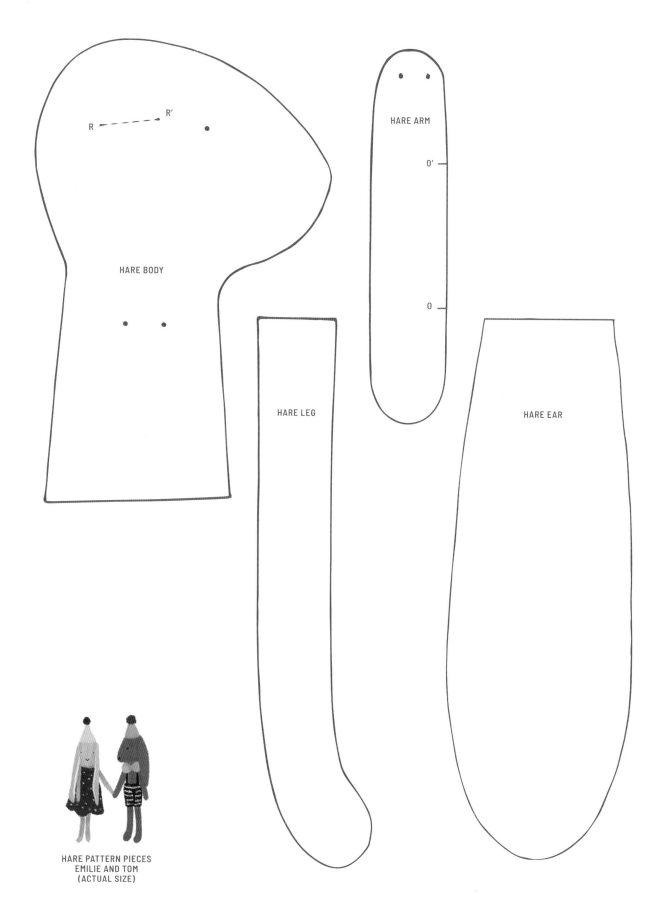

R ----- R'

HARE BODY

HARE ARM

O'

O

HARE LEG

HARE EAR

HARE PATTERN PIECES
EMILIE AND TOM
(ACTUAL SIZE)

Arthur and Lucile

MATERIALS

Finished size Arthur the dog: 27cm (10¾in) • Lucile the cat: 6.5cm (2½in) • The sun: 18 × 25cm (7 × 9¾in)
See page 174 for patterns.
For more details of the techniques used, see the Techniques section on page 10.

Arthur the dog
× 34 × 40cm (13½ × 15¾in) linen in sable
× 7 × 4cm (2¾ × 1½in) light-coloured, printed cotton
× 2 × 2cm (¾ × ¾in) felt in black
× 15 × 27cm (6 × 10¾in) velvet jersey in black
× 7 × 4cm (2¾ × 1½in) double-sided fusible interfacing
× 2.5 × 3.5cm (1 × 1½in) soluble fabric stabilizer
× Sewing thread, in black, sable and colours
to match your chosen printed fabric
× Toy filling
× 7 pattern pieces (body, head, ear, arm, tail, muzzle, nose)

The trousers
× 19 × 35cm (7½ × 13¾in) printed cotton
(or poplin, cretonne, polycotton)
× Sewing thread to match the chosen fabric
× 20cm (7¾in) flat elastic, 5mm (³⁄₁₆in) wide
× Safety pin
× 1 pattern piece (leg)

The tank top
× 5-ply (sport) cotton crochet yarn, in emerald green
× Crochet hook 3mm (UK 11, US 2/3)
× Marker ring
× Long pointed needle
× Stitches used: chain stitch (ch) • double
crochet (dc) • slip stitch (sl st)

The top hat
× 10 × 10cm (4 × 4in) felt in black
× Sewing thread in black
× Shirring elastic in gold
× 3 pattern pieces (top, brim, crown)

Lucile the cat
× 8 × 10cm (3¼ × 4in) cotton in ecru
× 2.5 × 2.5cm (1 × 1in) felt in pale pink
× Sewing thread in black, pale pink, blue and ecru
× Embroidery thread in metallic gold
× Toy filling
× Bell Ø 7mm (¾in)
× 2 pattern pieces (body, ear)

The sun
× 32 × 41cm (12½ × 16in) linen in mustard yellow
× 5 × 4cm (2 × 1½in) light-coloured, printed cotton
× 4 × 3cm (1½ × 1¼in) felt in black
× 5 × 4cm (2 × 1½in) double-sided fusible interfacing
× Sewing thread in black, mustard yellow and
colours to match the chosen printed fabric
× Nylon yarn
× 5 pattern pieces (sun pattern pieces
numbers 1 and 2, ray, muzzle, nose)

When your days become night, I will be there for you. I will chase away the shadows and my smile will bring back the blue sky... Because you are my ray of sunshine!

ARTHUR THE DOG

See the list of materials on page 160.

1 Following the cutting diagram, cut the linen into four pieces:
- 2 pieces 17 × 12cm (6¾ × 4¾in) for the head
- 2 pieces 26 × 14cm (10¼ × 5½in) for the body and the arms.

2 Following the cutting diagram, cut the velvet jersey into three pieces:
- 2 pieces 15 × 10cm (6 × 4in) for the ears
- 1 piece 15 × 7cm (6 × 2¾in) for the tail.

The face

3 Place the piece of soluble fabric stabilizer on the mouth drawn on the pattern piece for the dog's head. Trace and set to one side.

4 Place the fusible interfacing on the wrong side of the printed cotton. Fix with an iron.

5 On the wrong side of the printed cotton, namely the side with the interfacing, trace and cut out the shape of the muzzle. Peel off the protective backing from the fusible interfacing and set to one side for now (**a**).

6 Trace and cut out the shape of the nose from the black felt. Set to one side (**a**).

7 On the wrong side of one of the pieces of 17 × 12cm (6¾ × 4¾in) linen, trace the outline of the head, leaving a space of at least 1cm (⅜in) outside the line. Transfer markings A, B and C and the position of gap O–O'.

8 Transfer markings A, B and C to the right side of the fabric, using the pin method (see page 34).

9 Cut out the muzzle shape from the pattern piece for the head.

10 Place the head pattern piece on the right side of the piece of linen, using markings A, B and C to help (**b**).

11 Place the printed cotton muzzle in the hole you have cut out previously, with the fusible side against the linen (**c**). Carefully remove the pattern piece and press with an iron to hold the muzzle in place.

12 Set your sewing machine to zigzag stitch (stitch length: 0.5mm; stitch width: 2mm/1⁄16in). Sew around the outside of the muzzle, directly on the edge.

13 Place the felt nose on the muzzle, centred and 5mm (3⁄16in) from the bottom of the muzzle. Sew around the outside of the nose in straight stitch, 2mm (1⁄16in) from the edge, without oversewing at the start or finish.

14 Finish with the threads on the wrong side of the work and knot together. Snip off the excess.

15 Place the paper pattern on the right side of the face, according to the markings. Use a pin to mark the position of the eyes and the eyebrows (see technique on page 33) on the right side of the fabric.

16 Using doubled black thread, embroider a French knot for the eyes (see page 14).

17 Using a single black thread, embroider two small lines for the eyebrows.

18 Take the piece of soluble fabric stabilizer on which you traced the mouth and place it just under the nose. Pin to hold in place.

19 With the doubled black thread, embroider the mouth in backstitch over the line traced from the pattern, sewing through both layers of fabric (**d**).

20 Cut off the excess stabilizer around the embroidered mouth (**e**).

21 Put the embroidered portion of the face in some warm water for 1–2 minutes to dissolve the fabric stabilizer, then place it between two layers of towelling (terrycloth) and press so any excess water is absorbed.

Leave to dry.

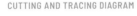

CUTTING AND TRACING DIAGRAM

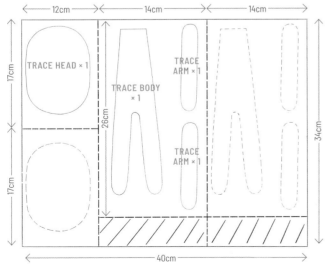

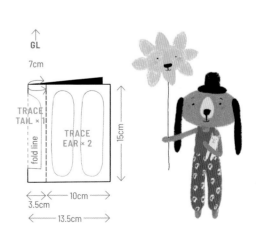

The body and the arms

22 On the wrong side of one piece of 26 × 14cm (10¼ × 5½in) linen, trace the following in accordance with the cutting diagram:

- the outline of the body × 1
- the outline of the arms × 2.

Leave a space of at least 1cm (⅜in) around the lines. Mark the position of gap O–O' for the arms.

23 Place this piece of fabric on the second piece of the same size, right sides together. Sew the pieces together along the lines, leaving open gap O–O', and at the top of the body marked with a red line on the pattern piece.

24 Trim the pieces 4mm (³⁄₁₆in) from the seams and directly against the opening in the body.

25 Clip the curves at the base of the legs and arms.

26 Turn each piece the right way out and stuff, pushing the toy filling well into the legs and body: they must be firm and hold their shape well. Put less toy filling in the arms so they remain flexible.

27 Turn under 4mm (³⁄₁₆in) from the edges of each gap. Sew up using slip stitch. Set to one side for now.

The ears

28 On the wrong side of one of the 15 × 10cm (6 × 4in) pieces of velvet jersey, trace the outline of the ear twice. Leave a seam allowance of at least 1cm (⅜in) around the lines. Mark the position of the gaps O–O'.

29 Place this piece of velvet jersey on the second piece of the same size, right sides together. Sew each of the pieces together, leaving gaps open.

30 Trim to 4mm (³⁄₁₆in) from the seams and the gaps.

31 Turn the ears the right way out.

32 Turn under 4mm (³⁄₁₆in) on either side of the gaps and sew up using slip stitch. Set to one side.

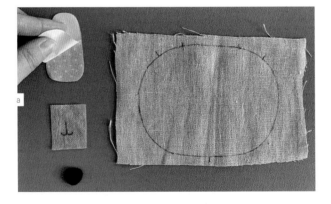

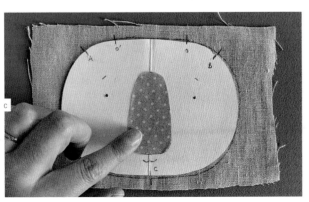

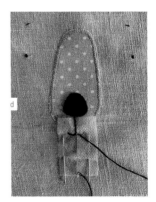

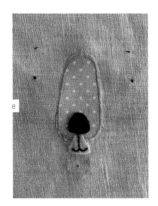

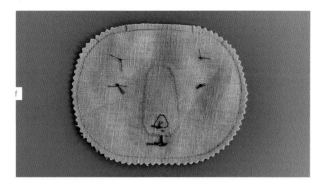

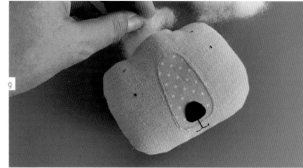

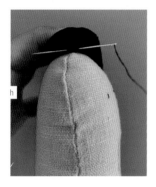

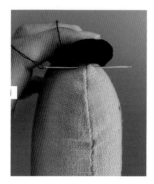

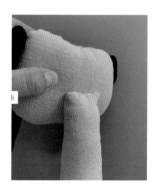

The tail

33 Fold the 15 × 7cm (6 × 2¾in) piece of velvet jersey in half lengthways, right sides together. Pin to hold in place.

34 Place the pattern piece for the tail on the piece of folded jersey: align the fold edge to edge. Trace the outline of the tail on the fold. Make sure you leave a margin of at least 1cm (⅜in) around the line.

35 Sew round the outline of the tail on the line, leaving the opening marked with a red line at the base of the tail unstitched.

36 Cut out the tail, 4mm (³⁄₁₆in) from the seam and directly against the gap. Turn the right way out and set to one side for now.

Assembling the head

37 Place the embroidered face on the second piece of linen of the same size, right sides together.

38 Sew round the head on the line marked, leaving gap O–O' open. Sew backwards and forwards a few times at the start and end of the seam to ensure the ends of the gap are secure.

39 Cut around the head, 4mm (³⁄₁₆in) from the seam and the gap. Clip the curves (**f**) and carefully turn the head the right way out.

40 Stuff firmly. Push the toy filling hard into the whole head so the curves are nicely rounded (**g**).

41 Turn under 4mm (³⁄₁₆in) on either side of the gap. Sew up using slip stitch.

Attaching the ears

42 Place one ear against the side of the head so the top of the ear is aligned with the top of the head. Centre the top of the ear on the seam between the front and back of the head.

43 Using doubled black thread, attach the ear to the head, inserting the needle alternately through the ear and through the head. Repeat this several times, oversewing in the same spot (**h**, **i**).

44 Do the same for the second ear.

Attaching the head

45 Position the front of the body against the back of the head, using the marking on the pattern to guide you.

46 Sew the head and the body together with slip stitch, using a single sable thread, sewing alternately through the head and the body. Leave the part under the chin unstitched. Sew backwards and forwards to ensure the seam is secure (**j**, **k**).

Attaching the arms

47 Position the arms on either side of the body in accordance with the marks. Using a needle threaded with doubled cordonnet crochet yarn, attach the arms on either side of the body, following the instructions on page 32.

Sewing on the tail

48 Turn under 4mm (³⁄₁₆in) on either side of the opening in the base of the tail.

49 Place the base of the tail against the dog's back, following the mark shown on the pattern piece.

50 Using a single black thread, sew on the tail using slip stitch, inserting the needle alternately through the edge of the top of the tail and through the dog's back.

The dog is complete! (l)

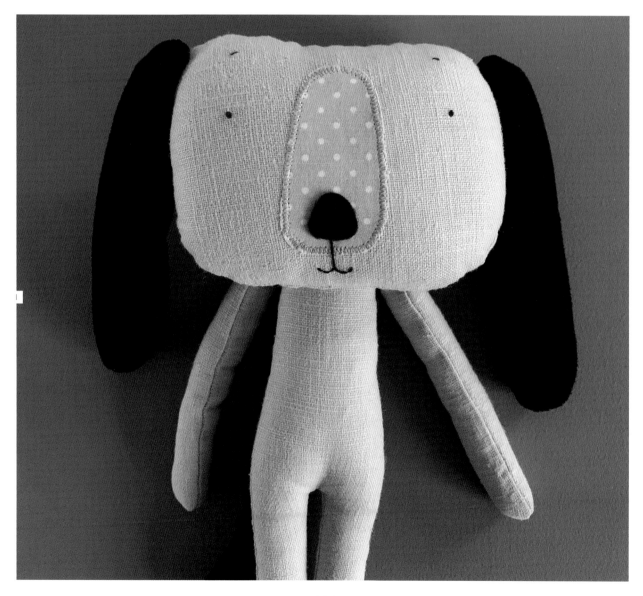

THE TROUSERS

See the list of materials on page 160.

CUTTING DIAGRAM

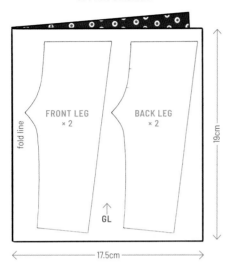

fold line

FRONT LEG
× 2

BACK LEG
× 2

GL

19cm

17.5cm

1 Cut out the pattern pieces for the trousers, following the instructions in the section Making fabric clothes on page 8.

2 Overcast the edges of all the pieces.

3 Place the two front pieces right sides together. Sew around the crotch, 5mm (³⁄₁₆in) from the edge. Iron open the seams and set to one side for now.

4 Place the two back leg pieces right sides together. Put in pins to mark O and O', marking the gap left for the tail.

5 Sew around the crotch, 5mm (³⁄₁₆in) from the edge, leaving the gap open. Press the seam open with an iron.

6 Place the front and back of the trousers right sides together. Sew along one long side, 5mm (³⁄₁₆in) from the edge. Press the seam open with an iron.

7 Turn the fabric at the top of the trousers under 1.2cm (½in) from the edge to form the waistband. Sew along the fold, 1cm (³⁄₈in) from the fold.

8 Insert the elastic into the waistband, using a safety pin to help, leaving the end sticking out 5mm (³⁄₁₆in) from the seam opening. Secure the start of the elastic by sewing across the open end of the hem, 3mm (⅛in) from the edge (**a**).

9 Pull on the other, unstitched end of the elastic, to reduce the width of the waist to 10cm (4in). Sew across the point where the elastic comes out of the waistband, 3mm (⅛in) from the edge, to secure the elastic in place (**b**). Cut off any excess elastic.

10 Sew along the second long side of the trousers, right sides together, 5mm (³⁄₁₆in) from the edge. Press the seam open with an iron.

11 Turn under 1cm (³⁄₈in) at the bottom of each trouser leg. Sew along the folds, 7mm (¼in) from the fold, to make the hems.

12 Sew right round the inside legs, 7mm (¼in) from the edge, right sides together. Turn the trousers the right way out.

The trousers are complete!

a

b

THE TOP HAT

See the list of materials on page 160.

1 On the wrong side of the piece of black felt, trace and cut out the three pattern pieces for the hat.

2 Right sides together, fold the rectangle of the crown of the hat in half widthways. Align the edges of the two shorter sides.

3 Sew the short edges together, 4mm (³⁄₁₆in) from the edge. Turn the tube you have obtained the right way out.

4 Position the small circle of the top of the hat at one end of the tube. Using a single black thread to sew them together, edge to edge, using straight stitch. You can insert a cotton reel, or another cylindrical object into the tube to support it as you sew (**a**).

5 Position the other end of the tube on the large circle of the hat brim (**b**). Centre it carefully. Sew them together with backstitch, inserting the needle a few millimetres above the edge of the tube, forming a small brim all around (**c**, **d**).

6 To attach, thread a needle with shirring elastic, and insert the needle through one side of the hat, following the markings shown on the pattern piece for the brim. Oversew two or three sides to hold the knot in place. Leave a 15cm (6in) length of elastic and sew through the other side of the hat. Tie a knot, sew over it a few times and work in the ends of elastic.

The top hat is complete!

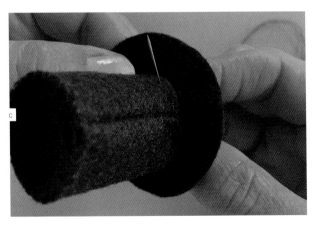

THE TANK TOP

See the list of materials on page 160.

The tank top

1 The tank top is worked in the round from the bottom up.

Round 1: ch 28, join into a ring with sl st.

Round 2: 1 dc in each st (= 28 sts).

Rounds 3–8: 1 dc in each st, only working in the back loop of the sts of the previous row (= 28 sts) (**a**).

End the work with 1 dc. Mark this st with the marker ring: this will be the central st for positioning the shoulder straps (**b**).

2 Work in the ends of the yarn.

The shoulder straps

3 Place the front of the tank top face up: the central st marked by the ring is at the back.

4 The shoulder straps start at the front of the body and are worked in rows.

First shoulder strap

Row 1: count 11 sts to the left from the central st. Starting at the twelfth st, work 3 dc (namely in the twelfth, thirteenth and fourteenth sts) (**c**).

Row 2: *flip work over, 1 ch 2 dc* (**d**).

Rows 3–12: rep from * to * (**e**).

Fasten off with 1 dc.

Second shoulder strap

Row 1: count 9 sts to the right from the central st.

From the tenth st, work 3 dc (namely in the tenth, eleventh and twelfth sts) (**f**).

Row 2: *Flip work over, 1 ch , 2 dc*.

Rows 3–12: rep from * to *.

Fasten off with 1 dc.

Finishing touches

5 Place the back of the tank top face up. Cross the straps and sew on each end with the working yarn, 1 st from each side of the central st (**g**).

6 Fasten off the yarn and snip off the excess (**h**).

The tank top is finished! Pull it on over the dog's legs before putting on the trousers.

LUCILE THE LITTLE CAT

See the list of materials on page 160.

The ears

1 On the wrong side of the piece of felt, trace and cut out the shape of the ear twice. Set to one side for now.

The body

2 Cut the cotton into two pieces 8 × 5cm (3¼ × 2in) for the front and back of the cat.

3 On the wrong side of one of the pieces of cotton, trace the outline of the body leaving a space of at least 1cm (⅜in) outside the line. Transfer the position of gap O–O' along with A–A' and B–B' marking the position of the ears.

4 Use a pin to mark the position of the eyes on the wrong side of the fabric (see technique on page 33). Use a pin to transfer markings 1, 2 and 3 to the wrong side of the fabric: the triangle formed by these three points will act as a guide for embroidering the nose and mouth.

5 Cut along the straight line marked at the top of the cat's head (**a**).

6 Using doubled blue thread, and without tying a knot, insert the needle at the position of one of the eyes, from the back to front of the fabric. Leave a good length of thread. Insert the needle again, in the right side of the fabric, just next to where it came out (**b**). Pull gently.

7 Knot together the ends of the thread on the wrong side of the fabric (**c**). Cut off the excess thread 2mm (¹⁄₁₆in) from the knot.

8 Do the same for the second eye.

9 Using a double thickness of pale pink thread, bring the needle up through mark 2, from the wrong side of the fabric (**d**). Using straight stitch, embroider horizontal stitches to fill the area of the triangle (**e**).

10 Using a single black thread, embroider the mouth starting at mark 3. It is up to you what sort of expression you want to give your little cat.

11 Using a single gold thread, embroider three straight stitches on each cheek for the whiskers, (**f**).

Assembling the body and ears

12 Place the embroidered fabric on the second piece of the same size, right sides together. Make sure it is properly centred between the top and bottom: the top edge should not be too close to the top of the head.

13 Start to sew around the outline of the body, starting from mark O'. When you are 4mm (³⁄₁₆in) from the cat's top edge, lift the presser foot of your sewing machine and place one ear, point down, between the two layers of fabric, between marks A–A'.

Carefully align the dotted line drawn on the pattern piece for the ear with the cutting line at the top of the head.

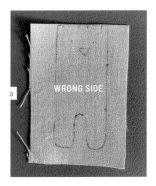

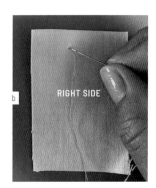

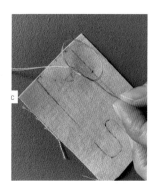

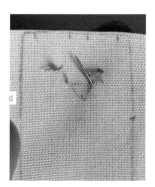

14 Sew along the top of the cat's head, 4mm (³⁄₁₆in) from the edge. When you reach mark B, lift the presser foot to insert the second ear and continue in the same way (**g**).

15 Continue along the line until you reach mark O (**g**).

16 Cut out the little cat, 3mm (⅛in) from the seam and the gap, avoiding the base of the ears where they stick out from inside the head. Clip the corners on either side of the top of the head (**h**).

17 Carefully turn the character the right way out, using a small tool (such as a paintbrush handle or a skewer): first bring out the ears then the arms and legs, one by one (**i**).

18 Stuff the little cat, starting with the legs.

19 Turn under 3mm (⅛in) on either side of the gap. Sew up using slip stitch.

Finishing touches

20 Thread the little charm on to a length of gold thread and tie it around the little cat's neck.

The little cat is complete!

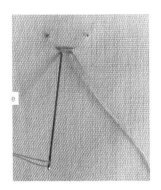
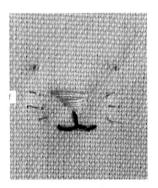
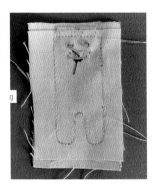
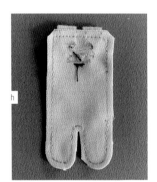

THE SUN

See the list of materials on page 160.

CUTTING AND TRACING DIAGRAM

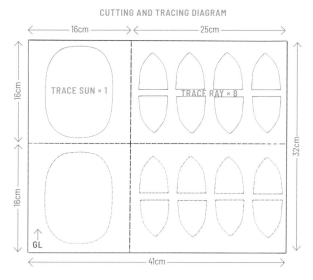

1 Following the cutting diagram, cut the linen into four pieces:
- 2 pieces 16 × 16cm (6¼ × 6¼in) for the front and back of the sun
- 2 pieces 16 × 25cm (6¼ × 9¾in) for the front and back of the rays.

The face

2 Place the fusible interfacing on the wrong side of the printed cotton. Fix with an iron.

3 On the wrong side of the printed cotton, the side with the interfacing, trace and cut out the shape of the muzzle. Peel off the protective backing from the fusible interfacing and set to one side for now.

4 Trace and cut out the shape of the nose from the black felt. Set to one side for now.

5 On the wrong side of one of the 16 × 16cm (6¼ × 6¼in) pieces of linen, trace the outline of the sun (pattern piece number 1), leaving a space of at least 1cm (⅜in) outside the line. Transfer markings A, B and C and the position of gap O–O'.

6 Transfer markings A, B and C to the right side of the fabric, using the pin method (see page 34).

7 Cut out the shape of the muzzle from pattern piece number 1, and place this pattern piece on the right side of the fabric, aligning it with markings A, B and C.

8 Place the printed cotton muzzle in the hole you have cut out, with the fusible side against the linen (**a**). Remove the pattern piece carefully. Press with an iron to hold the muzzle in place.

9 Set your sewing machine to zigzag stitch (stitch length: 0.5mm; stitch width: 2mm/¹⁄₁₆in). Sew around the outline of the muzzle, very close to the edge, starting at the bottom of the muzzle (**b**).

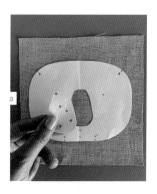

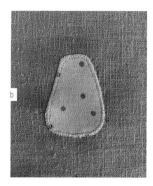

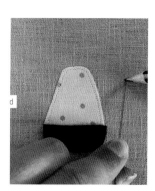

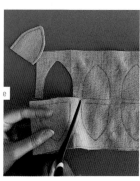

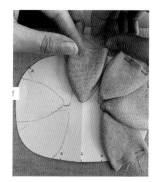

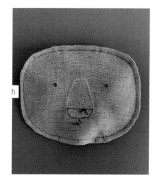

10 Place the felt nose on the bottom of the muzzle, aligning the shapes carefully. Sew around the outside of the nose in straight stitch, 2mm (1/16in) from the edge, without oversewing at the start or finish.

11 Finish with the threads on the wrong side of the work and knot together. Snip off the excess.

12 Place paper pattern number 1 on the right side of the face, aligning it with the markings. Use a pin to mark the position of the eyes on the right side of the fabric (**c**, **d**) (see the technique on page 33).

13 Using doubled black thread, embroider a French knot for the eyes (see page 14).

14 Using the black thread, still doubled, insert the needle on the wrong side of the face, under the muzzle, at point D (see pattern piece number 1). Embroider the mouth in backstitch, in the shape of a small arrow pointing downwards. Set to one side for now.

The rays

15 On the wrong side of one of the pieces of 16 × 25cm (6¼ × 9¾in) linen, trace the outline of the ray eight times, leaving a space of at least 1cm (⅜in) outside the lines, except at the base of the ray.

16 Place this piece of fabric on the second piece of the same size, right sides together.

17 Sew around each ray along the line, leaving the openings (at the base of the rays) open.

18 Cut around the rays, 4mm (3/16in) from the seams and directly against the openings (red line) (**e**).

19 Turn the rays the right way out, making sure you push out the points.

Assembling the sun

20 Position paper pattern number 2 on the embroidered face, aligning it with markings A, B, C.

21 Place seven rays on the pattern piece at the positions marked. Pin the base of the rays to the fabric of the face to hold them in position (**f**). Remove the pattern piece (**g**).

22 Place the embroidered face on the second piece of 16 × 16cm (6¼ × 6¼in) linen, right sides together.

23 Sew around the sun along the lines, removing the pins as you reach them. Leave the gap open. Sew backwards and forwards a few times at the start and end of the seam to ensure the ends of the gap are secure.

24 Cut around the sun, 4mm (3/16in) from the seam and the gap (**h**).

25 Turn the sun the right way out, pulling the rays out gently, one by one.

Finishing touches

26 Stuff the sun. Push the toy filling hard up against the seams so the curves are nicely rounded.

27 Turn under 4mm (3/16in) on either side of the gap.

28 Insert the base of the eighth ray approximately 5mm (¼in) into the gap.

29 Using a single yellow thread, sew up the gap using slip stitch, inserting the needle alternately in the fold on either side and through the head.

30 Sew a small length of nylon thread to the back of the sun at markings N and N' shown on pattern piece number 2.

31 Knot the ends and snip off the excess thread.

The sun is complete!

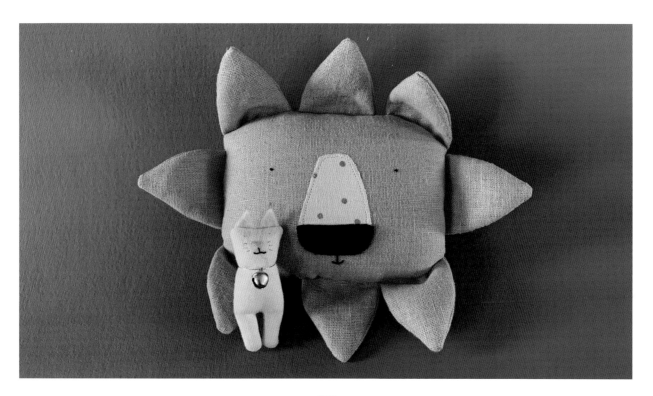

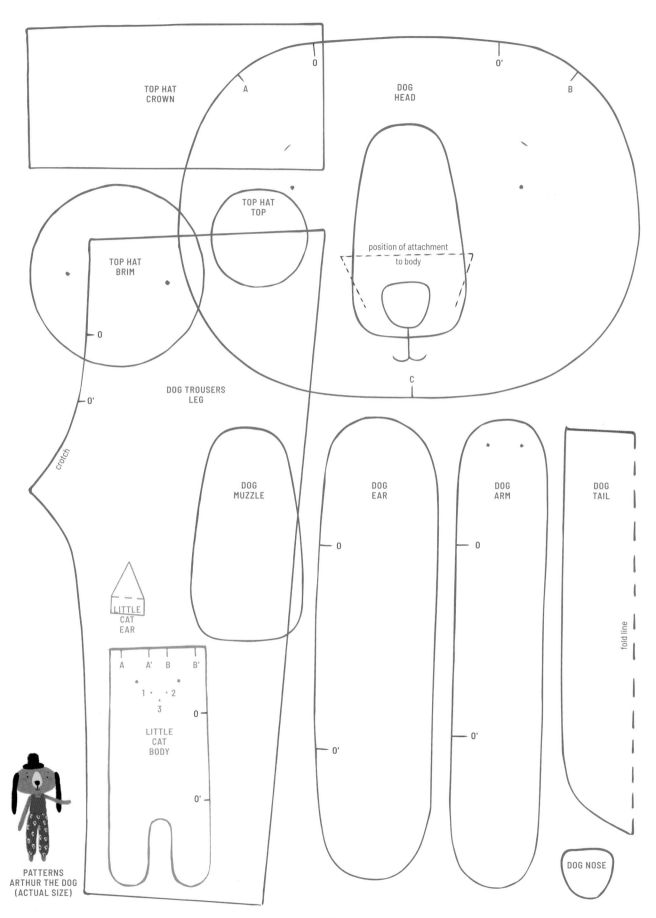

TOP HAT
CROWN

DOG
HEAD

A

0

0'

B

TOP HAT
TOP

TOP HAT
BRIM

0

position of attachment
to body

0'

crotch

C

DOG TROUSERS
LEG

DOG
MUZZLE

DOG
EAR

DOG
ARM

DOG
TAIL

0

0

fold line

LITTLE
CAT
EAR

0

0'

A   A'   B   B'

1 • • 2
    •
    3

LITTLE
CAT
BODY

0

0'

DOG NOSE

PATTERNS
ARTHUR THE DOG
(ACTUAL SIZE)

174

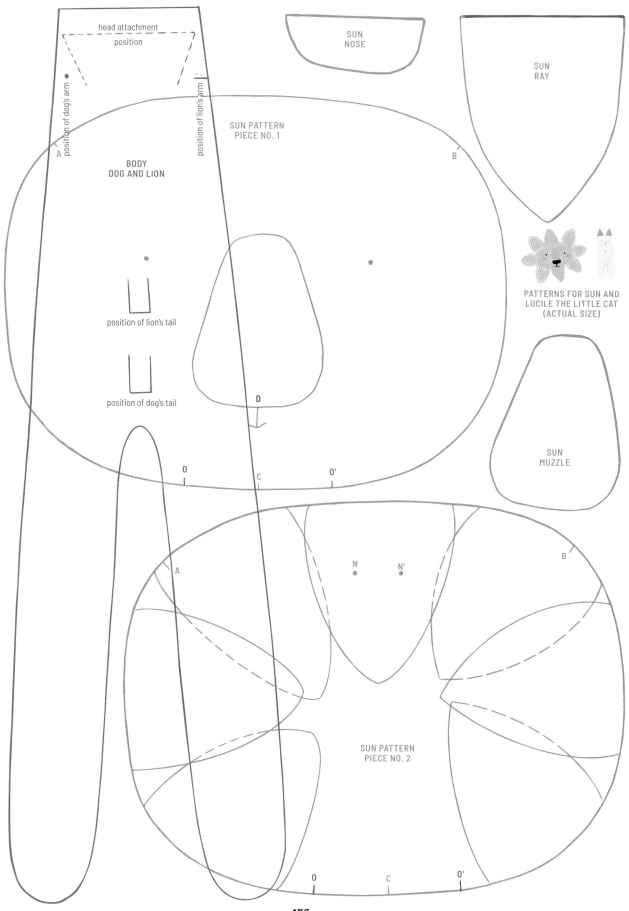

head attachment
position

position of dog's arm

position of lion's arm

BODY
DOG AND LION

A

SUN PATTERN
PIECE NO. 1

B

position of lion's tail

position of dog's tail

D

O   C   O'

SUN
NOSE

SUN
RAY

PATTERNS FOR SUN AND
LUCILE THE LITTLE CAT
(ACTUAL SIZE)

SUN
MUZZLE

A   B

N   N'

SUN PATTERN
PIECE NO. 2

O   C   O'

175

Acknowledgements

I owe the warmest of thanks to the Éditions Eyrolles team: Aude Decelle, Anaïs Nectoux, Mélissa Morey, Sophie Hincelin and Armelle Mancini, without whom this book would never have seen the light of day. Their willingness to listen and their advice have been a great help to me. How many hours have we spent together on the phone, Anaïs? Many thanks also to Lauriane Tiberghien for her beautiful layout.

Thank you to my mum, who taught me to knit when I was nine and who would (patiently or otherwise) pick up the stitches that I clumsily dropped.

Thank you to Nanny Nénette, who worked magic with her needles and repaired the whole family's rips and tears: she was the epitome of patience and attention to detail.

Thank you to Monique, my mother-in-law, who helped me take my first steps in crochet one Saturday afternoon many years ago.

Thank you to Granny Jacquotte, my beloved grandma, for always letting me rummage through her things and use her sewing kit for my Wednesday crafts. Thank you to her for having kept everything I made and for actually displaying a few in the glass cabinet in her sitting room!

Many thanks to all the people who passed on their knowledge and techniques via creative tutorials, workshops and books: not everyone is lucky enough to have a talented grandmother to hand!

Thank you to the young illustrators: you are a source of inspiration to me.

Many thanks to everyone who supports my work with little words of encouragement; the confidence they showed in me was a great support. Rose Minuscule exists thanks to them!

Thank you to the few people who knew that I was writing this book: they were with me every step of the way, happy to listen or give advice when I was in doubt. I love you!

Finally, a very special thank you to Malou, who wrote a few of the sentences in this book. Some were cut and do not appear in full in the final version of the book, but I shall write them out again in full, faithfully and proudly, on my Instagram feed.

And thank you to you, dear readers, for having chosen this book. I hope you find beauty and joy everywhere around you!